California
Winery Tours

 Automobile Club of Southern California

Cover photo—James Blank

Writer, Michelle S. De Lude • **Graphic Artist,** Barbara Stanfield

Editor, Judy van Wingerden • **Editorial Assistant,** Patricia Vaquero

Although information presented in this publication has been carefully researched and was as accurate as possible at press time, the Automobile Club of Southern California is not responsible for any changes or errors which may occur. When practical, it is wise to verify information immediately prior to your visit.

Only attractions or establishments that are approved by an Automobile Club of Southern California field representative may advertise. The purchase of advertising, however, has no effect on inspections and evaluations. Advertisements provide readers with additional information that may be useful in selecting what to see and where to stay.

Additional advertisements (excluding attractions and establishments) for travel-related services may also be included in ACSC publications. Acceptance of these advertisements does not imply endorsement by ACSC.

ISBN: 1-56413-182-3
Printed in the United States of America

Copyright © 1993 by Automobile Club of Southern California
Travel Publications Department
2601 South Figueroa Street, Los Angeles, California 90007

Contents

INTRODUCTION 7

CALIFORNIA WINE HISTORY 9

CALIFORNIA WINES 11

WINERY LISTINGS 13

SOUTHERN CALIFORNIA 14
    Map 14
    Annual Events 15
    Escondido Area 16
    Temecula Area 16
    Los Angeles and San Bernardino Counties 18

CENTRAL COAST 20
    Annual Events 20
    Map 21
    Ventura and Santa Barbara Counties 22
        Ventura 22
        Santa Barbara 23
        Lompoc 23
        Buellton 23
        Solvang 24
        Santa Ynez 24
        Los Olivos 24
        Santa Maria 26
    San Luis Obispo County 26
        Nipomo 26

Arroyo Grande 26
San Luis Obispo...27
Creston 28
Templeton 28
Paso Robles 28
San Miguel...30

MONTEREY TO SAN FRANCISCO BAY AREA 31
  Map 31
  Map 32
  Annual Events 33
  Monterey and San Benito Counties 34
    Greenfield..34
    Soledad 34
    Gonzales...35
    Hollister 35
  Santa Cruz County 35
  Santa Clara County 37
    Gilroy...37
    Morgan Hill 39
    San Jose..39
    Los Gatos 39
    Saratoga 40
    Cupertino..40
  Eastern San Francisco Bay Area...........................40
  Western San Francisco Bay Area 42

**MENDOCINO, LAKE AND NORTHERN
SONOMA COUNTIES** 44
  Map 44
  Map 46
  Annual Events 47
  Northern Sonoma County 48
    Santa Rosa Area, including the cities of Sebastopol, Occidental
    Forestville, Fulton, and Guerneville 48
    Windsor 50
    Healdsburg 51
    Geyserville 56
    Cloverdale 58
  Mendocino County 58
    Hopland..58
    Philo..59
    Ukiah...61

    Redwood Valley...62
  Lake County..62
    Kelseyville, Lakeport and Lower Lake 62

NAPA AND SONOMA VALLEYS 63
  Annual Events 63
  Map 64
  Map 65
  Napa Valley..67
    Napa Area...67
    Yountville Area 70
    Oakville Area 73
    Rutherford Area 74
    St. Helena Area..78
    Calistoga Area 83
  Sonoma Valley and Southern Sonoma County 86
    Sonoma..86
    Glen Ellen...88
    Kenwood...89
    Santa Rosa Area 90

CENTRAL VALLEY 91
  Map 92

SIERRA FOOTHILLS 93
  Annual Events 93
  Map 94
  California State Highway 99 95
  Calaveras County...96
  Amador County 98
  El Dorado County..99
  Nevada County 100

GLOSSARY OF WINE TERMS 102

INDEX OF WINERIES 106

INDEX TO ADVERTISERS 110

GET EVERYTHING FOR YOUR TRIP. FREE.

Fee-Free American Express® Travelers Cheques

Maps, TourBooks® & Area Guides

Car Rental Reservations & Discounts

AIRLINE TICKETS

Complete Airline & Travel Reservations

Hotel/Motel Reservations & Discounts

Dependable Emergency Road Service

Join the Auto Club of Southern California today and we'll give you everything you need for your trip. ✦ Free maps ✦ Free TourBooks®, CampBooks® and area guides ✦ Fee-free American Express® Travelers Cheques and ✦ Free Triptiks®, a personalized, mile-by-mile routing of your entire trip. And you'll love saving money with Member-only discounts on ✦ Tours and cruises ✦ Hotel/motel reservations ✦ Rental cars and ✦ Popular attractions across the country. All of these great travel benefits can be yours for $38 a year plus a $20 enrollment fee -- a total of just $58. So why wait? Join AAA today and get everything for your trip. <u>Free</u>!

Call 1-800-882-5550, Ext. 147 (Outside So. CA: 1-800-AAA-HELP)

Associate memberships for your spouse and children are available for a nominal fee. Membership dues are subject to change without notice.

Introduction

Why tour a winery?

Winemaking is a family endeavor. Although multinational conglomerates may own a few of the famous-name wineries, often—in the case of Mondavi, for instance, or Gallo—the wineries are still operated by the founders or their families. Visit a winery and you will often come face to face with California history across the tasting bar or in the cellars and caves. Immigrant Europeans of the 19th century saw images of their homeland etched into the state's coastal valleys. The Beringer family went so far as to build a replica of their Bavarian home on the hillsides of St. Helena. In addition to the landscape that resembled parts of Italy, France and Germany, California's Mediterranean climate proved conducive to grape growing. If you screen out the modern tourist-oriented trappings of today's Napa Valley—where traffic is heavy even on a rain-swept winter weekend—you may gain a glimpse of Bordeaux, Tuscany or Alsace.

This book describes many California wineries offering tours to individuals and small groups. (Wineries open only for tasting and sales are listed separately.) Some wineries, such as Beringer and Mondavi, take groups on rehearsed, timed tours. Others, such as Arciero and

St. Supéry, provide well-marked, informative self-guided tours. At still others, such as Storrs Winery, Black Sheep Vintners and Caparone, the tasting room and winery are housed in the same building: no trying to keep up with the group as it descends into dark, humid caves or walking down aisles of tanks in hangar-sized storage areas. Fetzer, in Hopland, has a spectacular organic vegetable garden; Ferrari-Carano, Peju Province and Justin Vineyards have lovely flower gardens; Deer Park Escondido, Perry Creek and Arciero exhibit classic automobiles and race cars; the Hess Collection and Clos Pegase house their owners' art collections and double as private art museums.

If tours are given by appointment, be sure to call or write the winery at least a week ahead of your intended visit. Even if no appointment is required, it is advisable to call the wineries on your itinerary in advance. Special events can change regular schedules. Some wineries use their facilities for weddings or other private events that preclude uninvited visitors; public concerts, festivals or special tastings may cause traffic delays and parking difficulties. Advance arrangements should always be made for group visits; many wineries will schedule private tours and tastings for large parties of tourists.

The fall harvest is the busiest time of year, and September and October provide the best opportunity to see the full range of winemaking operations. Many of the smaller wineries cannot accommodate visitors at this time, however, because staff members cannot take time away from their other duties. Winter, the quietest season, is a good time to avoid crowds. Activity gradually resumes in spring and summer, when the vineyards need tending and the tourist season gets under way.

Besides touring the winery itself, visitors can learn about the effects of various winemaking techniques through tasting. Tasting and drinking are two different activities, and some wineries charge a nominal fee for tasting to discourage those hoping for a free before-dinner drink. Tastings, or "Sensory evaluations," are really just a specialized version of "show-and-tell." Tasting room staff members are educators, not bartenders, and often can provide a wealth of information not only about the wines they pour, but about the background of the winery, local history and many other subjects. How does the color and taste differ between a Cabernet, Zinfandel, Pinot Noir and Merlot? How does Chardonnay taste when it has been fermented in stainless steel instead of oak? How do grapes grown on the valley floor differ from those grown on a steep mountainside?

How should you transport the wine you purchase during your travels? The best solution usually is to have the winery ship it to your home, but wine can only be shipped to states that have reciprocal trade agreements with California: Colorado, Idaho, Illinois, Missouri, New Mexico, Oregon, Washington and Wisconsin. If you want to transport the wine yourself, store the wine in the coolest part of your car, out of direct sunlight and on its side. Adequate padding will prevent bottle breakage;

make sure bottles and wine glasses are positioned so they won't bounce against hard surfaces. Styrofoam wine shippers for single and double bottles are ideal and can be purchased at many mailing outlets. When you arrive home, let the bottle sit a day or two before opening. Wine may taste a bit "off" if opened immediately after a rough journey or cross-country shipping.

Many travelers enjoy visiting several wineries in a day's journey. It's a good idea to eat a good meal before setting out. Keep in mind that food and fuel are found primarily in downtown areas or along major highways such as SR 29 and US 101. Winemaking is primarily an agricultural endeavor, and towns are sometimes separated by miles of vineyards and not much else. If a winery has a deli, cafe or refrigerated items for sale, it will be noted in the listing. To help you locate wineries in the same vicinity, this book is divided into seven major geographic regions: Southern California, Central Coast, Monterey to San Francisco Bay Area, Mendocino, Lake and Northern Sonoma Counties, Napa and Sonoma Valleys, Central Valley, and Sierra Foothills. Within these regions, destinations are listed from south to north and grouped by city or town. This book also contains ten regional maps showing winery locations.

Throughout this book, references are given to maps published by the Automobile Club of Southern California and the California State Automobile Association that cover these areas in detail. ACSC publications cover the southern part of California, and some are available for retail sale; CSAA publications cover the northern part of the state and are available exclusively to AAA members. (For more information on AAA membership, call your nearest AAA-affiliated office.)

California Wine History

California's original winemakers were Spanish missionaries led by Father Junípero Serra. As they moved north from Baja California, founding their chain of 21 missions, they planted a succession of vineyards. From what became known as the Mission grape, the Franciscans produced a wine that was adequate for sacramental, medicinal and table use.

For nearly 60 years, the missionaries were California's only viticulturists. Then, in the 1820s, commercial wine growing was launched in the Los Angeles area. Joseph Chapman, the first commercial grower, was followed a decade later by Jean Louis Vignes, a Frenchman who brought vine cuttings with him from Europe. Soon these pioneers had competitors. The Gold Rush brought an increased demand for wine, and with it, an influx of European winemakers. Krug, Mirassou, Korbel, Beringer, Martini, Concannon—the mixed heritage of California's wine industry is reflected in the names of its founders.

Among the immigrant viticulturists was a Hungarian named Agoston Haraszthy. Like Jean Louis Vignes, he brought European grape varieties to Southern California. In 1857 he moved to Sonoma, where his vinifera vines thrived. Subsequently, Haraszthy was commissioned by the state's governor, John G. Downey, to tour Europe and return with reports of winegrape cultivation and winemaking practices there. When he returned, he brought more cuttings from the vineyards of Europe. His work, along with that of families such as Mirassou, fostered the conversion of California vineyards from the Mission grape to premium Old World varieties such as Cabernet Sauvignon and Chardonnay.

California's progress was almost completely reversed by a dreaded plant louse, phylloxera. This pest was discovered in England in 1863; by the end of the century it had virtually destroyed the vineyards of France and caused widespread damage in other European countries. California got its first hint of danger in 1874, when a vineyard in Sonoma County was found to be afflicted by the pest. Soon phylloxera was devastating the vines of Sonoma, Napa, Yolo, El Dorado and Placer counties. Finally a remedy was discovered. By grafting the fragile European grapevines to sturdier American rootstock, the vineyards could be saved. It meant replanting nearly every vineyard, both in America and Europe, but it salvaged the wine industry. Paso Robles and Amador County are two areas that were never afflicted by the louse, and some very old pre-phylloxera vines still survive there.

Not long after California's vineyards recovered from phylloxera, Prohibition dealt its blow. A few wineries were able to survive by producing medicinal and sacramental wines; most went out of business. Grape growers fared better; because home winemakers were allowed to produce 200 gallons annually, there was still a strong market for grapes.

After 13 years, Prohibition was finally repealed, but the industry's troubles were not over. The sudden demand for wine could not be met—except, in part, with inferior or even synthetic wines. California winemakers were in danger of losing their market, as well as their reputation. As a means of self-protection, they founded the Wine Institute, which in turn convinced the government to establish quality and labeling standards for wines sold in the United States.

At last the wine industry was back on its feet. The quality of California wines, as well as the demand for them, was higher than ever before. Despite two wine depressions, California winemaking experienced steady overall growth from the 1930s to the 1960s. Since then, the industry has fared even better thanks to a rapidly expanding market.

Large corporations have enjoyed a substantial share of the wine boom. The largest, E & J Gallo, produces four times as much wine as any other corporation in the United States. Corporate names are behind some of the more widely distributed labels, including Fetzer, Beaulieu and Beringer. Although the benefits of corporate control are widely debated, the big companies have helped meet the demand for inexpensive table wines.

Small, premium wineries—those concentrating on a few varietal wines produced in limited quantity—have also prospered; their number increases each year. Many have won international recognition in prestigious tastings and competitions.

There were predictions that California's wine industry would reach its peak in the mid-1970s. Instead, it continued to expand. In most of the state's viticultural regions, many new wineries have begun operations during recent years, and advances in winemaking techniques and the increasing quality of California fruit have drawn international attention and a vast amount of foreign investment during the 1980s. Many prominent wineries are now owned by French, German, Japanese, British, Swiss and Spanish concerns. Dimming the recently bright reputation of California wines and causing uncertainty about its future is a new type of phylloxera that has been discovered attacking the state's vineyards, economic troubles that closed many wineries in the early 1990s, problems created by tourism and land development that have given rise to zoning and building restrictions limiting winery and vineyard expansion, and continuing debates over how to balance the health benefits and risks involved in drinking different kinds of alcoholic beverages.

California Wines

There are two main categories of California wines: varietal and generic. In accordance with current laws, varietal wines contain at least 75 percent of one grape variety (such as Cabernet Sauvignon), and they are labeled with the name of that grape. Generic wines, on the other hand, can be made from almost any blend of grapes. If the terms generic and varietal are unfamiliar, associating them with "general" and "variety" may help keep them straight. Although inexpensive generic wines may bear labels like "Chablis" or "Burgundy" (which are, strictly speaking, areas of France, as are Champagne and Bordeaux), a small group of winemakers has developed a keen interest in the classic Bordeaux-type blends. This kind of wine is sometimes referred to as Meritage or "claret," and fine examples can be found at Cosentino, Cain, and Robert Sinskey, among others.

Vintage date and origin also help identify wines. A date on the label indicates that at least 95% of the wine is from grapes harvested that season. This enables you to recognize wines produced in good years, when the climate has been particularly favorable, and to avoid the occasional vintage that may have suffered from excessive heat or early rain. (But don't forget that great wines can be made in "poor" years.) Another signpost of quality is the name of a premium growing region, like Napa Valley, on the label. When these American viticulture areas (AVA) appear on the label, it indicates the origin of at least 85 percent of the grapes in a wine.

If you intend to serve wine with a meal, you will probably want a table wine. This most familiar type has an alcohol content of between 7 and 15 percent. It may be red, white or pink (rosé). Red wines, which tend to be dry and full-bodied, are generally served with red meats and other hearty foods. White table wines are more delicate and range from dry to sweet; they are often enjoyed by themselves as well as with meals (particularly fish, fowl and light meat dishes), and the sweetest varieties go well with dessert. Rosé wines, served with almost any dish, are especially suited to casual dining. Modified according to your own preferences, these guidelines will help you select a wine that complements your meal.

Sparkling wines are table wines that have undergone a second fermentation to make them effervescent. The most popular is styled after French Champagne and is labeled according to its sweetness: Natural is extremely dry, with Brut, Extra Dry and Sec progressively sweeter.

Aperitif and dessert wines have a higher alcohol content, between 17 and 21 percent. Served before meals, aperitif wines include dry sherry and vermouth. Sweet sherries, port and numerous late-harvest varietals are considered dessert wines, to be served after meals.

Unlike the other categories, fruit and berry wines are not produced from grapes but from other types of fruit, such as strawberries, apricots or cherries. They tend to be sweet, with an alcohol content that is generally 12 percent but may be as high as 20 percent.

Winery
Listings

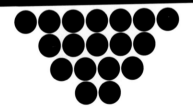

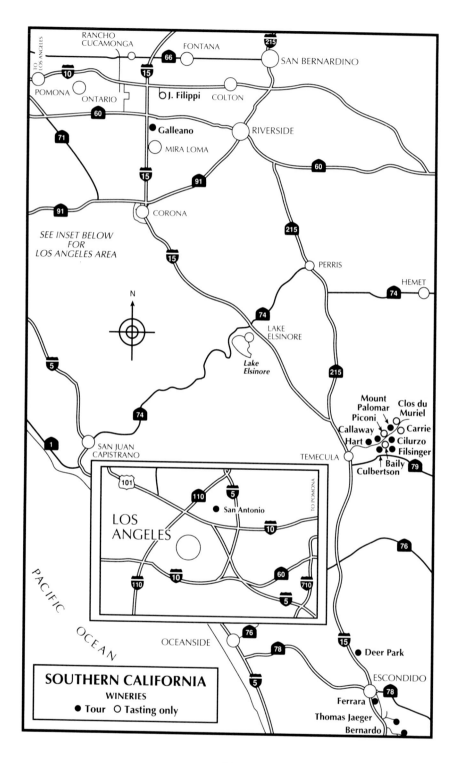

SOUTHERN CALIFORNIA
WINERIES
● Tour ○ Tasting only

Southern California

Southern California was once the center of California winemaking. In 1769 missionaries planted their first vineyard at Mission San Diego; 70 years later, grape growing was the major industry in the Los Angeles area. The city's steady growth gradually overtook the vineyards, but several of the original wineries have remained in operation.

The warm climate and sandy soil of the Cucamonga Valley were well suited to inexpensive grape varieties such as Zinfandel and Mission. Vineyards, however, eventually gave way to suburban sprawl. Meanwhile, new plantings are being cultivated near Temecula, where the cooler temperatures are more suitable for premium grapes such as Cabernet Sauvignon and White Riesling. Farther south, just a few hundred acres of vineyards remain in the Escondido district.

ANNUAL EVENTS

Exact dates, prices and other information about the events listed below may be verified by calling the telephone numbers shown. Some wineries also individually sponsor special brunches, dinners and summer concerts. Those interested in the events sponsored by a particular winery should call that winery and ask if a calendar of events is available.

FEBRUARY—

Loyola Marymount University Wine Classic *Los Angeles.* (310) 338-3065. Wine tasting provided by more than 45 premium California wineries. The $50 admission includes a souvenir wine glass, wine tasting, buffet of cheeses, pates, fruits and breads.

Barrel Tasting *Temecula.* (909) 699-3626. Wine from the barrel is paired with gourmet foods and hors d'oeuvres at participating wineries. Tickets to this two-day, valley-wide event include a commemorative glass. Telephone the Temecula Valley Vintners' Association at the above number, or write them at P.O. Box 1601, Temecula 92390.

MAY—

Temecula Balloon and Wine Festival *Lake Skinner, Temecula.* (909) 676-6713. Hot air balloons are launched and wine tastings take place throughout the weekend. Hot air balloon rides are given to those with reservations. Food and beverage booths, arts and crafts exhibits, live entertainment and a Kids' Faire round out the family atmosphere. Reserve a balloon ride and order tickets ($10) from the Temecula Valley Balloon & Wine Association at 27475 Ynez Road, Suite 335, Temecula, CA 92591 or telephone number above.

JULY—

Wine & Jazz *Temecula* at Baily Vineyard & Winery. (909) 695-1895.

NOVEMBER—

Nouveau Celebration *Temecula.* (909) 699-3626. This valley-wide event celebrates the release of the nouveau wines, poured for the first time and paired with gourmet foods. Call the number above or write the Temecula Valley Vintners' Association, P.O. Box 1601, Temecula 92390.

ESCONDIDO AREA

BERNARDO WINERY 7 mi SE of Escondido off Pomerado Rd at 13330 Paseo del Verano Norte, San Diego 92128. (619) 487-1866. Open daily 9 am to 3 pm for tasting and self-guided tours. Patio restaurant open Tuesday through Sunday, 11 am to 5 pm. (See ACSC *North San Diego Area* map, F-19.)

Bernardo, founded in 1889 and located in a complex of art, gift and specialty shops, is the oldest winery in San Diego County. The original wood aging vats are still in use, and the winery has maintained its producing vineyards. All Bernardo wines—dessert and table—are sold exclusively through the retail store on the premises.

DEER PARK ESCONDIDO 1 mi S of Gopher Canyon Rd at 29013 Champagne Bl, Escondido 92026. (619) 749-1666. Open daily 10 am to 5 pm for tasting. Museum open daily 10 am to 4 pm; admission $4 adults, $2 seniors, children under 12 free. (See ACSC *Oceanside-Escondido Area* map, E-17.)

This tiny facility produces only 450 cases of Chardonnay per year from its three-and-a-half-acre vineyard, and the crushing and pressing equipment used in production is similarly small-scale. A three-building complex houses winery owner Robert Knapp's collection of convertible automobiles dating from 1903 to 1976 and the winery operations. Several picnic areas are located throughout the grounds, and refrigerated deli items are sold in the spacious tasting room.

FERRARA WINERY 1120 W 15th Av, Escondido 92025. (619) 745-7632. Open weekdays 9 am to 5:30 pm, weekends 10 am to 5:30 pm, for tasting and self-guided tours. (See ACSC *Oceanside-Escondido Area* map, R-22.)

The Ferrara Winery is located on a five-acre plot on the west side of Escondido. Founded in 1932 and appointed a State Historical Point of Interest in 1971, the facility blends traditional and contemporary motifs: old redwood tanks contrast with a modern stainless steel stemmer-crusher. The Ferrara family produces both varietal and generic wines, which can be sampled in the tasting room.

THOMAS JAEGER WINERY 6 mi SE of Escondido via I-15 and Via Rancho Pkwy at 13455 San Pasqual Rd, San Diego 92025. (619) 738-6500. Open daily for tasting, 10 am to 6 pm summer, to 5 pm rest of year. Tours daily at 11:30 am, 1:30, 3 and 4 pm. (See ACSC *North San Diego Area* map, C-19.)

Paul Thomas and the Jaeger family of Rutherford Hill and Freemark Abbey bought the former San Pasqual Vineyards in 1988. The winery produces about 13,000 cases each year of an assortment of varietal wines. There is a shaded picnic arbor, indoor tables for use during inclement weather, and picnic items are sold in the gift shop.

TEMECULA AREA

CALLAWAY VINEYARD & WINERY 4 mi E of Temecula at 32720 Rancho California Rd, Temecula 92390. (909) 676-4001. Open daily 10:30 am to 5 pm for tasting; $3 fee includes souvenir glass. Tours weekdays at 11 am, 1 and 3 pm; weekends from 11 am to 4 pm, every hour on the hour. (See ACSC *Murrieta-Temecula Area* map, K-12.)

The Callaway Winery's original 1969 vineyard was planted to take advantage of cool coastal breezes and a microclimate suitable for premium grape production; it now consists of 720 acres. Constructed four years later, the winery was designed to incorporate modern equipment and techniques, explained in the informative daily tours. There is a gift shop, refrigerated deli items and picnic facilities.

CILURZO VINEYARD AND WINERY 5.5 mi E of Rancho California off Rancho California Rd at 41220 Calle Contento, Temecula 92592. (909) 676-5250. Open daily 9:30 am to 4:45 pm for tasting and self-guided tours; $1 tasting fee refunded with purchase. (See *Murrieta-Temecula Area* map, K-23.)

Vincenzo and Audrey Cilurzo bought their Temecula property in 1967 as a haven from Vincenzo's high-pressure Hollywood career, and in 1978 they began making wine. Annual production ranges between 8000 and 10,000 cases per year; four white and three red varietals, a chianti-style proprietary blend and a late-harvest Petite Sirah make up the current offerings of the Cilurzos and winemaker Larry Evilsizer. A tree-shaded picnic area overlooks a small lake with ducks.

CULBERTSON WINERY 32575 Rancho California Rd (PO Box 9008), Temecula 92390. (909) 699-0099. Open daily 10 am to 5 pm for tasting; fee $6. Tours weekends only. Cafe Champagne open daily 11 a.m. to 9 p.m. (See ACSC *Murrieta-Temecula Area* map, L-21.)

The Culbertson's home winemaking, grocery, and cafe in Fallbrook evolved into this impressive stone and slate facility in the Temecula Valley, with a restaurant and shaded picnic area across the courtyard from the winery. Now owned by John Thornton, the 40,000-case-per-year winery is the only Southern California winery specializing in méthode champenoise sparkling wine.

FILSINGER VINEYARDS 11 mi E of Temecula off SR 79 at 39050 De Portola Rd, Temecula 92592. (909) 676-4594. Open weekends 10:30 am to 5 pm for tasting; $1 fee. Tours by appointment. (See ACSC *Murrieta-Temecula Area* map, J-27.)

William Filsinger comes from a family of German wine makers, and in 1972 he renewed his ties to that part of his heritage by purchasing this property in Temecula and planting vines. The winery was built eight years later, and today it produces Cabernet Sauvignon, Chardonnay, Gamay Beaujolais, Gewürztraminer, Johannisberg Riesling, Sauvignon Blanc and white Zinfandel. In 1990, Filsinger released its first sparkling wines, which are made using the méthode champenoise. Winery production is about 8000 cases per year. Visitors may picnic at the shaded tables adjacent to the tasting room.

HART WINERY 4 mi E of Temecula at 41300 Avenida Biona (PO Box 956), Temecula 92593. (909) 676-6300. Open daily 9 am to 4:30 pm for tasting; $2 fee. Tours on request. (See ACSC *Murrieta-Temecula Area* map, K-21.)

This small family winery was built in 1980 adjacent to an 11-acre vineyard. Cabernet Sauvignon, Chardonnay, Grenache, Merlot, Mourvedre, Sauvignon Blanc and White Riesling are produced from estate-grown and purchased grapes.

MOUNT PALOMAR WINERY 5 mi E of Temecula at 33820 Rancho California Rd, Temecula 92591.(714)

676-5047. Open daily 9 am to 5 pm for tasting; fee includes souvenir glass. Tours weekdays at 1:30 and 3:30 pm; on weekends at 11:30 am, 1:30 and 3:30 pm. (See ACSC *Murrieta-Temecula Area* map, K-23.)

Mount Palomar was one of the first wineries established in the Temecula area. In 1969, John Poole sold his broadcasting business, left Los Angeles, and planted the vineyards here; the winery was constructed in 1975. Today, the winery produces 15,000 cases per year of a wide range of varietals, including Cabernet Sauvignon, Chardonnay, Chenin Blanc, Johannisberg Riesling, Sauvignon Blanc, white Cabernet and white Zinfandel. Guided tours are given daily at 1:30 and 3:30 p.m., with an 11:30 a.m. tour added on weekends. A nominal fee for tasting includes a souvenir glass. The full-service deli is open Friday through Sunday, and other picnic items can be purchased daily. Visitors are invited to use the picnic tables.

Wineries Open For Tasting Only

The following wineries in the Temecula area have tasting rooms on the premises but do not offer tours.

BAILY VINEYARD & WINERY

36150 Pauba Rd, Temecula 92592. (909) 676-9463. Open weekends 10 am to 5 pm. (See ACSC *Murrieta-Temecula Area* map, L-26.) Second tasting room at 33833 Rancho California Rd, Temecula, CA 92591. (714) 695-1895. Open daily 10 am to 5 pm. $1 tasting fee refunded with purchase and picnic facilities at each location.

MAURICE CARRIE WINERY

34225 Rancho California Rd, Temecula 92591. (909) 676-1711. Open daily 10 am to 5 pm. Gift shop, refrigerated deli items, picnic area and children's playground. (See ACSC *Murrieta-Temecula Area* map, K-23.)

CLOS DU MURIEL

40620 Calle Contento, Temecula 92591. (909) 676-2938. Open daily 10 am to 5 pm. Gift shop, $1 tasting fee. (See ACSC *Murrieta-Temecula Area* map, J-23.)

JOHN PICONI VINEYARD & WINERY

33410 Rancho California Rd, Temecula 92591. (909) 676-5400. Open daily 10 am to 5 pm except major holidays. Gift shop, $2 tasting fee includes souvenir glass. (See ACSC *Murrieta-Temecula Area* map, K-22.)

LOS ANGELES AND SAN BERNARDINO COUNTIES

GALLEANO WINERY

4231 Wineville Rd, Mira Loma 91752. (909) 685-5376. Open for tasting Mon through Sat 9 am to 6 pm, Sun 10:30 am to 5 pm. Tours Sun at 3:30 and 4 pm, and by appointment. (See ACSC *Pomona-Ontario Area* map, P-22.)

Galleano Winery has been a family enterprise since it was established in 1933. Galleano's list features wines of almost every variety: aperitif, table, dessert and sparkling. There is a gift shop, refrigerated deli items and a picnic area.

SAN ANTONIO WINERY, INC.

737 Lamar St, Los Angeles 90031. (213) 223-1401. Open for tasting daily 10:30 am to 6 pm except major holidays. Tours 10 am to 2 pm every hour on the hour. (See ACSC *Guide to Metropolitan Los Angeles*, G-10.)

Santo Cambianica founded his winery in 1917 in what is now the industrial district of Los Angeles. Today it is a thriving family business offering a variety of wines including varietal wines made from grapes from Napa and Sonoma counties and the Central Coast. There is a gift shop, and a restaurant on the premises serves northern Italian and continental dishes which can be enjoyed inside or in the winery's tree-shaded park.

Winery Open For Tasting Only
The following winery in the San Bernar-

dino-Redlands area has a tasting room on *the premises but does not offer tours.*

J.FILIPPI VINTAGE CO. 1.25 mi S of I-10 at 11211 Etiwanda Av at Jurupa Av in Fontana (PO Box 2), Mira Loma 91752. (714) 428-8630. Open daily 9 am to 6 pm. Gift shop, refrigerated deli items, picnic facilities. (See ACSC *San Bernardino-Redlands Area* map, P-3.)

Central Coast

The Central Coast is a designated viticultural area that includes San Luis Obispo, Santa Barbara and Ventura counties, among others. San Luis Obispo and Santa Barbara counties were important wine producing areas a century ago, and the region has again become very popular. The University of California at Davis discovered conditions ideal for the growth of premium grape varieties in Santa Barbara County, especially Chardonnay, Riesling and Pinot Noir. Today, there are more than 30 wineries in the Santa Barbara County, which has an active vintners association that sponsors county-wide events in the spring and fall. The Santa Ynez Valley, a sub-appellation of the Central Coast, lies within Santa Barbara County; the Santa Maria Valley is divided between Santa Barbara and San Luis Obispo counties.

A similar boom in viticulture has occurred in San Luis Obispo County. The favorable climate, with sea breezes and fogs moderating summer temperatures, has combined with good soil and land availability. A number of new operations are demonstrating the region's suitability for premium wine production. The county also boasts some of the oldest California wineries, which have traditionally emphasized Zinfandel and generic table wines. Designated viticultural areas within the county include the Edna Valley, Paso Robles and York Mountain.

ANNUAL EVENTS

Exact dates, prices and other information about the events listed below may be verified by calling the telephone numbers shown. Some wineries also individually sponsor special brunches, dinners and summer concerts. Those interested in the events sponsored by a particular winery should call that winery and ask if a calendar of events is available.

APRIL—

Santa Barbara County Vintners' Festival various locations and events in Santa Barbara County. Two days of food and wine tasting along with musical entertainment. Tickets are $50 and must be ordered in advance by writing the Vintners' Association at P.O. Box 1558, Santa Ynez 93460, or calling (805) 688-0881.

Santa Ynez Valley Carriage Classic *Los Olivos*. (805) 688-4454, 688-3940. Held at Firestone Winery meadow.

Equestrian show and competition, food and beverage booths, picnic.

MAY—

Paso Robles Wine Festival *Paso Robles*. (805) 238-0506 or (800) 322-5471. Weekend of jazz bands and wine tasting in the park; $15 includes souvenir glass and a number of tasting tickets. Food and jazz events at wineries and downtown events also scheduled. Winemaker dinners require separate reservations and tickets. Call the Chamber of Commerce at the number above or write them at 1225 Park Street, Paso Robles 93446.

JUNE—

Ojai Wine Festival *Lake Casitas*. (800) 648-4881, (805) 646-5747. Crafts, local restaurants, wineries, cooking demonstrations, educational seminars, live music. One-day ticket costs $15 and includes souvenir glass and a number of tasting tickets. Call number above or

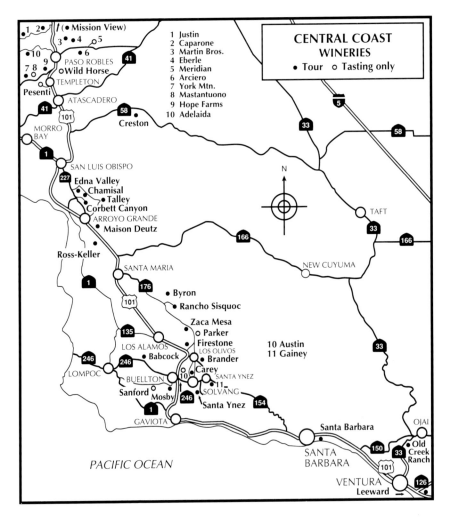

CENTRAL COAST
WINERIES
• Tour   o Tasting only

1 Justin
2 Caparone
3 Martin Bros.
4 Eberle
5 Meridian
6 Arciero
7 York Mtn.
8 Mastantuono
9 Hope Farms
10 Adelaida

write Ojai Wine Festival, P.O. Box 1320, Oak View 93022.

JULY—
KCBX Central Coast Wine Classic
San Luis Obispo and Santa Barbara counties. (805) 781-3026. Barrel tasting, reception, dinners at various restaurants and wineries, winery luncheons and tours, auction, brunch, wine tasting. Ticket prices vary. Call or write 4100 Vachell Lane, San Luis Obispo 93401.

Blues Festival *Buellton* Mosby Winery at Vega Vineyards. (805) 688-2415. $20 ticket includes commemorative glass, glass of wine and full afternoon of blues.

AUGUST—
Museum Wine Festival *Santa Barbara* at Santa Barbara Museum of Natural History. (805) 682-4711. The woods along Mission Creek at the museum provide the setting for this event featuring wine, food and music from the county's

vintners, caterers and restaurants. The $35 tickets must be ordered in advance.

SEPTEMBER—

Central Coast Wine Festival *San Luis Obispo.* (805) 546-4231 for 24-hour hotline or (805) 541-1721. 50 wineries participate in this event at Mission Plaza which includes a live band, food booths, wine tasting and other booths with wine-related items and information. Tickets are $25 and may be ordered in advance from the Arthritis Foundation at the number above.

OCTOBER—

A Celebration of Harvest *Santa Barbara County.* A one-day celebration of the county's vintners, farmers and ranchers. Wine and food tasting, including a wide variety of produce from throughout the county; musical entertainment. Order tickets in advance from the Vintners' Association, P.O. Box 1558, Santa Ynez 93460, or call (805) 688-0881.

Morro Bay Harbor Festival *Morro Bay.* (805) 772-1155. Seafood fair and barbecue gives visitors a chance to talk one-on-one with the commercial fishermen as they barbecue mussels, oysters, albacore and other seafood. Events include Cal Poly rowing team in rowing regatta, maritime heritage pavilion with historical exhibits, arts and crafts, live music and entertainment. Top seafood restaurants team up with local wineries to provide tasting samples. Tickets cost $2 for adults; children under 12 are free.

NOVEMBER—

Harvest Celebration Arroyo Grande and Edna Valley. (805) 541-5868. More than a dozen local wineries meet and pour their wines, including older "library" vintages and wine from barrels. Food, live music, vineyard tour and auction. Tickets $35.

Winery Open House *Ventura* at Leeward Winery. (805) 656-5054. All wines opened for tasting, reds and whites in different parts of the winery. Vertical tastings; fruit and vegetable snacks provided.

Beaujour Celebration *Santa Barbara* at Santa Barbara Winery. (805) 963-3633, (800) 255-3633.

DECEMBER—

Christmas Open House *Buellton* at Mosby Winery at Vega Vineyards. (805) 688-2415. Wine tasting, food sampling, Christmas carols.

Christmas Open House *Santa Ynez* at The Gainey Vineyard. (805) 688-0558.

Open House *Paso Robles* at Eberle Winery. (805) 238-9607. Live music, appetizers, barrel tasting.

VENTURA AND SANTA BARBARA COUNTIES

VENTURA

LEEWARD WINERY 2784 Johnson Dr, Ventura 93003. (805) 656-5054. Open daily 10 am to 4 pm for tasting and tours. (See ACSC *Ventura County* map, L-4.)

This small winery opened in 1979 in an unlikely location at Oxnard's Channel Islands Harbor; it moved to its present site in mid-1982. The owners purchase select lots of Cabernet Sauvignon, Chardonnay, Pinot Noir and Merlot grapes from Northern and Central California vineyards; production is currently 15,000 cases annually.

OLD CREEK RANCH WINERY 1.5 mi S of Oak View at the end of Old Creek Rd (PO Box 173), Oak View 93022. (805) 649-4132. Open for tasting Fri through Sun 10 am to 4 pm.

Tours by appointment. (See ACSC *Ventura County* map, J-3.)

Old Creek Ranch lies along the banks of San Antonio Creek, and although a winery was built around the turn of the century, today's winery has been operation only since 1981. Grapes from Santa Maria Valley and Ventura County go into six types of varietal wine produced here at the southern end of Ojai Valley. Visitors who wish to tour the facility should call ahead for an appointment.

SANTA BARBARA
SANTA BARBARA WINERY 202
Anacapa St, Santa Barbara 93101. (805) 963-3633, (800) 225-3633. Open daily 10 am to 5 pm for tasting. Tours daily at 11:30 am, 3:30 pm and by appointment. (See ACSC *Santa Barbara County* map, city inset, K-12.)

Santa Barbara Winery was launched by Pierre LaFond in 1962, making it the oldest producing winery in Santa Barbara County. A selection of the wines can be sampled in the winery's tasting room.

LOMPOC
BABCOCK VINEYARDS 7 mi E of
Lompoc at 5175 SR 246, Lompoc 93436. (805) 736-1455. Open weekends 10:30 am to 4 pm or by appointment for tasting and tours. (See ACSC *Santa Barbara County* map, G-5.)

Winemaker Bryan Babcock produces about 8000 cases per year of Chardonnay, Gewürztraminer, Pinot Noir, Riesling, Sauvignon Blanc and Sangiovese from 50 acres of estate vineyards and from other vineyards in Santa Barbara County. This small family winery sits at the western edge of the Santa Ynez Valley district in the Purisima Hills, not far from La Purisima Mission State Historic Park. Walter and Mona Babcock also own two restaurants in Orange County in addition to the winery. There is a shaded picnic area, and portions of the long driveway to the winery are steep and unpaved.

BUELLTON
MOSBY WINERY AT VEGA
VINEYARDS off US-101 at 9496 Santa Rosa Rd (PO Box 1849), Buellton 93427. (805) 688-2415. Open daily 10 am to 4 pm; $2.50 tasting fee. Tours by appointment only. (See ACSC *Santa Barbara County* map, G-6.)

Bill and Jeri Mosby planted their vineyard on what was once part of the Rancho de la Vega, a 19th-century land grant. They converted the old carriage

house into a winery and in 1979 crushed their first vintage there. Today the Mosby family produces wine from estate-grown and purchased grapes. Varieties include not only Chardonnay, Riesling, Gewürztraminer and Pinot Noir, but also the Italian varieties Brunello, Nebbiolo, Primativo and Pinot Gris. Visitors are welcome to picnic.

Winery Open For Tasting Only

The following winery in Buellton has a tasting room on its premises but does not offer tours.

SANFORD WINERY 4 mi W of Buellton at the 11.78 mile marker, 7250 Santa Rosa Rd, Buellton 93427. (805) 688-3300. Open daily 11 am to 4 pm. (See ACSC *Santa Barbara County* map, G-5.)

SOLVANG

CAREY CELLARS 2 mi E of Solvang off SR 246 at 1711 Alamo Pintado Rd, Solvang 93463. (805) 688-8554. Open daily 10 am to 4 pm for tasting and tours. (See ACSC *Santa Barbara County* map, G-7.)

The winery founded by the Carey family in 1978 was purchased by Firestone Vineyards (near Los Olivos) nine years later. Along with Cabernet Sauvignon, Merlot, and Sauvignon Blanc from the estate La Cuesta and Alamo Pintado vineyards in the Santa Ynez Valley, winemaker Alison Green makes Chardonnay and Pinot Noir in the renovated old barn. A shaded picnic area is available to visitors.

SANTA YNEZ

THE GAINEY VINEYARD 1 mi E of Santa Ynez at 3950 E SR 246 (PO Box 910), Santa Ynez 93460. (805) 688-0558. Open daily 10 am to 5 pm for tasting and tours; $2.50 tasting fee

includes souvenir glass. (See ACSC *Santa Barbara County* map, G-8.)

This modern winery was designed and built with the visitor in mind. Informative tours thoroughly cover all phases of winemaking, beginning in the vineyard and proceeding through crushing, fermentation, laboratory, barrel and bottle aging to the tasting room. The adjacent 64-acre vineyard will eventually produce all of the fruit for the winery's 15,000-case-per-year, five-varietal output. A summer concert series is held each year.

SANTA YNEZ WINERY 343 N Refugio Rd, Santa Ynez 93460. (805) 688-8381. Open daily 10 am to 5 pm for tasting and self-guided tours. (See ACSC *Santa Barbara County* map, G-7.)

The Old College Ranch was dairy land for over 50 years, until conversion to vineyards began in 1969. The first crush, in 1976, yielded 500 cases. Now the remodeled barn is used to make 18,000 cases of wine annually. Emphasis is on white varietals, including Sauvignon Blanc, Chardonnay and Riesling, all from the winery's 110-acre vineyard. Picnic facilities are available, and from June through September the winery sponsors a series of twilight dinners (reservations are necessary).

LOS OLIVOS

BRANDER VINEYARD 2 mi SE of Los Olivos off SR 154 (PO Box 92), Los Olivos 93441. (805) 688-2455. Open daily 10 am to 5 pm for tasting. Tours by appointment. (See ACSC *Santa Barbara County* map, G-7.)

The 40-acre Brander Vineyard was planted in 1975, and the winery was built five years later. Now 8000 cases annually of estate-bottled varietals are produced under the Brander label; the

Michelle De Lude

Equestrian events take place in a vineyard setting during the Santa Ynez Valley Carriage Classic, held in April at Firestone Vineyard.

emphasis is on the house specialty, Sauvignon Blanc and Bordeaux-type blends. A second label is used for non-estate-bottled wine.

FIRESTONE VINEYARD 8 mi N of Buellton via US 101 on Zaca Station Rd (PO Box 244), Los Olivos 93441. (805) 688-3940. Open daily 10 am to 4 pm for tasting and tours. (See ACSC *Santa Barbara County* map, F-7.)

In 1973, Brooks Firestone (of the tire manufacturing family) planted vines near Los Olivos, a region offering climatic conditions similar to those of the Napa Valley. The first harvest occurred in 1975, and current bottlings include Riesling, Gewürztraminer, Sauvignon Blanc, Chardonnay, Merlot and Cabernet Sauvignon. Picnic facilities are also available.

ZACA MESA WINERY 15 mi N of Buellton via US 101 and Zaca Station Rd on Foxen Canyon Rd (PO Box 899), Los Olivos 93441. (805) 688-3310. Open daily 10 am to 4 pm for tasting. Tours every hour on the half hour. (See ACSC *Santa Barbara County* map, E-7.)

In 1973 Zaca Mesa Ranch converted 160 acres of grazing land to vineyard. A new winery was finished in time for the 1978 harvest. Now 213 acres of vineyards produce the fruit for 36,000 cases of wine each year. Zaca Mesa offers estate-bottled Chardonnay, Pinot Noir and Syrah. There is a tasting room, gift shop, and an adjacent shaded picnic area.

Wineries Open For Tasting Only

The following wineries in Los Olivos have tasting rooms on the premises but do not offer tours.

AUSTIN CELLARS 2923 Grand Av (PO Box 636), Los Olivos 93441. (805) 688-9665. Open daily 11 am to 6 pm late May through early Sep, to 5 pm rest of year. (See ACSC *Santa Barbara County* map, G-7.)

PARKER WINERY 5 mi E of jct US 101 and Zaca Station Rd at 6200 Foxen Cyn Rd (PO Box 908), Los Olivos 93441. (805) 688-1545. Open daily 10 am to 4 pm. (See ACSC *Santa Barbara County* map, F-7.)

SANTA MARIA

BYRON VINEYARD & WINERY 12 mi SE of Santa Maria at 5230 Tepusquet Rd, Santa Maria 93454. (805) 937-7288. Open daily 10 am to 4 pm for tasting and tours; closed major holidays. (See ACSC *Santa Barbara County* map, D-6).

Byron Vineyard & Winery crushed its first vintage in 1984 under winemaker Byron "Ken" Brown. The winery focuses its efforts on Chardonnay and Pinot Noir and produces limited quantities of Cabernet Sauvignon and Sauvignon Blanc. All grapes are estate grown or purchased from vineyards in the Santa Maria and Santa Ynez valleys. In 1989, Byron acquired the Nielson Vineyard, the county's oldest commercial vineyard, and last year, an 18-acre experimental vineyard was planted. This high-density vineyard has three times the vines per acre usual in California. The tasting room and cellar are made from knotty pine, and a landscaped picnic area is available to visitors.

RANCHO SISQUOC WINERY 22 mi N of Buellton via US 101 and Zaca Station Rd on Foxen Canyon Rd (Rt 1, Box 147), Santa Maria 93454. (805) 934-4332. Open daily 10 am to 4 pm for tasting and tours. (See ACSC *Santa Barbara County* map, D-6.)

Rancho Sisquoc is a huge cattle ranch in the foothills of the San Rafael Mountains near the Sisquoc River. The entrance to the ranch is marked by the San Ramon Chapel, and cattle and quail can be seen along the one-lane dirt road that winds its way to the winery. A small portion of the ranch has been planted to grapes, with the first crush in 1972. Commercial winemaking began in 1977 when the winery was bonded; now 5000 cases of varietal wines are bottled yearly. A number of picnic tables are scattered about the open lawn next to the tasting room.

SAN LUIS OBISPO COUNTY

NIPOMO

ROSS-KELLER WINERY 985 Orchard Av, Nipomo 93444. (805) 929-3627. Open daily for tours and tasting, noon to 5 pm from Apr through Nov, Wed through Sun noon to 5 pm rest of year. (See ACSC *San Luis Obispo County* map, H-8 or *Santa Barbara County* map, B-3.)

Ross-Keller's owners are horse breeders, and the winery is situated on their Standardbred ranch. About 3000 cases per year of several red and white varietals are made from locally grown purchased grapes. Visitors are welcome to use the winery's picnic area.

ARROYO GRANDE

MAISON DEUTZ WINERY 1 mi S of Arroyo Grande off US 101 at 453 Deutz Dr, Arroyo Grande 93420. (805) 481-1763. Open for tasting daily except Tue, 11 am to 5 pm; $3.75 to $5 tasting fee includes appetizers. Closed major holidays. Tours by appointment only. (See ACSC *San Luis Obispo County* map, H-7.)

The venerable French Champagne house of Deutz founded their California outpost in 1981 on the rolling hills south of Arroyo Grande. Vineyards of Pinot Blanc, Pinot Noir and Chardonnay were planted, and a modern gravity-flow winery was constructed. Sparkling wines alone are vinified, and only by the traditional méthode champenoise.

TALLEY VINEYARDS 350 yds N of Orcutt Rd at 3031 Lopez Dr, Arroyo Grande 93420. (805) 489-0446. Open for tasting daily 11 am to 5 pm Memorial Day through Sep 15, Thu through Sun 11 am to 5 pm rest of year. Tours by appointment. (See ACSC *San Luis Obispo County* map, G-7.)

Oliver Talley began growing specialty vegetables in the Arroyo Grande Valley in the late 1940s. In 1982, the Talley family moved into viticulture and planted a test plot that has grown into 102 acres in three separate vineyards; the new winery was finished in 1991. Production is less than 5000 cases per year of Sauvignon Blanc, white Riesling, and the winery's specialties, Chardonnay and Pinot Noir. Visitors may sample the wines in the Rincon Adobe, built in the 1860s. There is a wide lawn, a gazebo, and several large round picnic tables.

San Luis Obispo

CHAMISAL VINEYARD 7525 Orcutt Rd, San Luis Obispo 93401. (805) 544-3576. Open Wed through Sun 11 am to 5 pm for tasting and tours. (See ACSC *San Luis Obispo County* map, G-7.)

This Edna Valley facility produced its first wine—a Chardonnay—in 1980. Previously, grapes from the 57-acre vineyard adjacent to the mission-style stucco winery were sold to several Northern California concerns. The Goss family markets approximately 3000 cases of their wines.

CORBETT CANYON VINE-YARDS 8 mi SE of San Luis Obispo off SR 227 at 2195 Corbett Canyon Rd (PO Box 3159), San Luis Obispo 93403. (805) 544-5800. Open weekdays 10 am to 4:30 pm, weekends 10 am to 5 pm. Tours weekends at 11 am, 1 and 3 pm, and by appointment. (See ACSC *San Luis Obispo County* map, G-7.)

The first winery in the southern half of San Luis Obispo County commenced operations in 1979. Now, at more than 300,000 cases per year, it is the largest of the county wineries. In addition to Cabernet Sauvignon, Sauvignon Blanc and white Zinfandel, Corbett Canyon Vineyards also produces estate Chardonnay and Pinot Noir. There is a gift shop and art gallery, and deli items and a picnic area are available.

EDNA VALLEY VINEYARDS 5 mi SE of San Luis Obispo off SR 227 at 2585 Biddle Ranch Rd, San Luis Obispo 93401. (805) 544-9594. Open daily 10 am to 4 pm. (See ACSC *San Luis Obispo County* map, G-7.)

The drought of 1976 and 1977 forced Chalone Inc. to purchase grapes to supplement their harvest. They bought from Paragon Vineyards of San Luis Obispo. In 1980, the two businesses joined together to build the winery at Edna Valley Vineyard. The focus is on Chardonnay; Pinot Noir is also grown along with some Vin Gris and Napa Gamay, and sparkling wine is made in addition to table wine. All 700 acres of vineyards are adjacent to this 50,000 to 60,000 case-per-year winery. Tables are available for picnics in the herb garden, and tours cover the entire winemaking process.

CRESTON

CRESTON VINEYARDS on SR 58 at 17 milepost; Hwy 58, Star Rte, Creston 93432. (805) 238-7398. Templeton tasting room open daily 10 am to 5 pm. Tours and tasting at winery by appointment only. (See ACSC *San Luis Obispo County* map, E-9.)

Larry and Stephanie Rosenbloom bought the Indian Creek Ranch in 1980, and in 1982 they began building a winery on the 479-acre property. Set high in the La Panza mountains, the area still looks and feels like ranchland, but vineyards can clearly be seen from the offices. Creston Vineyards produces about 30,000 cases per year of a large number of varietal wines. The road winds narrowly in spots and is not recommended for trailers. The tasting room at the winery is at the convergence of three roads down the hill from the offices; a second tasting room, open daily, is located in Templeton at SR 101 and Vineyard Drive, (805) 434-1399.

TEMPLETON

YORK MOUNTAIN WINERY 9 mi W of Templeton via SR 46 on York Mountain Rd; Rt 2, Box 191, Templeton 93465. (805) 238-3925. Open daily 10 am to 5 pm for tasting; closed major holidays. Tours by appointment only. (See ACSC *San Luis Obispo County* map, D-5.)

Max Goldman bought this winery, originally established in 1882, as a retirement investment after more than 51 years in the winemaking business. Pinot Noir, Chardonnay, Cabernet Sauvignon and Zinfandel are vinified from the win-

ery's eleven acres, and are available for sale and tasting along with Merlot, sherry, port, sparkling wine and generic wine. The original winery building houses the tasting room.

Wineries Open For Tasting Only
The following wineries in the Templeton area have tasting rooms on their premises but do not offer tours.

MASTANTUONO WINERY 4 mi W of Templeton at corner of Vineyard Dr and SR 46; 100 Oak View Rd, Templeton 93465. (805) 238-0676. Open daily 10:30 am to 6 pm May through Oct, 10 am to 5 pm rest of year. Picnic facilities available. (See ACSC *San Luis Obispo County* map, D-5.)

PESENTI WINERY 3 mi W of Templeton at 2900 Vineyard Dr, Templeton 93465. (805) 434-1030. Open Mon through Sat 8 am to 6 pm, Sun 9 am to 6 pm. Gift shop. (See ACSC *San Luis Obispo County* map, D-6.)

WILD HORSE WINERY 5 mi E of Templeton off Templeton Rd (PO Box 910), Templeton 93465. (805) 434-2541. Open weekdays by appointment for tasting and sales. (See ACSC *San Luis Obispo County* map, D-6.)

PASO ROBLES

ADELAIDA CELLARS 5.5 mi off Nacimiento Lake Dr at 5805 Adelaida Rd, Paso Robles 93446. (805) 239-8980. Open daily 10:30 a.m. to 4:30 p.m. for tasting and tours. Second tasting room located at Sycamore Farms Natural Herb Farm on SR 46, 3 mi E of US 101; open daily 10:30 am to 5:30 pm, (805) 238-5288.

John Munch crushed his first vintage in 1981 using leased facilities. It took him four moves and another ten years to finally build his own winery. He produces Cabernet Sauvignon, Chardonnay and Zinfandel, all from low-yield mountain vineyards west of Paso Robles in San Luis Obispo County. Munch prefers to work with fruit from dry-farmed vineyards and believes winemaking has more in common with cooking than chemistry; his rich, intensely flavorful wines attest to his philosophy. An amphitheater on Fair Oaks Mountain above the winery provides a setting for musical entertainment and special dinners. Munch's wife, Andree, also makes wine: Le Cuvier wines may be tasted at the Sycamore Farms tasting room.

ARCIERO WINERY 6 mi E of Paso Robles on SR 46 (PO Box 1287), Paso Robles 93447. (805) 239-2562. Open daily for tasting and tours 10 am to 5 pm, to 6 pm on summer weekends. (See ACSC *San Luis Obispo County* map, C-7.)

This modern estate winery of Mediterranean design was built in 1986 in the rolling foothill country east of Paso Robles. The facility, which can be examined on self-guided tours, overlooks more than 500 acres of estate vineyards. Nine varietal wines are produced; these can be sampled daily in the tasting room. Five acres of landscaping includes a rose garden, fountain and picnic area. The Arciero family's retired race cars are on exhibit. Refrigerated picnic items are for sale in the gift shop and the winery hosts concerts during the summer.

CAPARONE 1.5 mi off Nacimiento Lake Dr (County Hwy G12) at 2280 San Marcos Rd, Paso Robles 93446. (805) 467-3827. Open daily 11 am to 5 pm for tasting and tours. (See ACSC *San Luis Obispo County* map, C-6.)

Dave Caparone makes only unfiltered, unfined red wines—Brunello, Cabernet Sauvignon, Merlot, Nebbiolo and Zinfandel—of intense varietal character. Processing is limited to racking, a laborious, time-consuming and traditional method of clarifying wine. Visitors may taste unreleased wines from the barrel as well as current releases, and they will find the in-depth tours approachable, entertaining and flexible.

EBERLE WINERY 3.5 mi E of Paso Robles on SR 46 (PO Box 2459), Paso Robles 93447. (805) 238-9607. Open daily for tasting 10 am to 6 pm May through Sep, to 5 pm rest of year. Tours by appointment. (See ACSC *San Luis Obispo County* map, C-6.)

Gary Eberle's modern wooden winery sits atop a small rise just east of Paso Robles. The 12,000-case annual production of Chardonnay, Cabernet Sauvignon, Muscat Canelli, Barbera, Syrah and Zinfandel is made primarily from estate-grown grapes. The large tasting room is designed so that visitors can oversee the winery floor through bay windows.

HOPE FARMS WINERY 1 mi W of US 101 on SR 46 at 2175 Arbor Rd (PO Box 3260), Paso Robles 93447. (805) 238-6979. Open daily 11 am to 5 pm for tasting; $2 fee includes souvenir glass. Closed major holidays. Tours by appointment. (See ACSC *San Luis Obispo County* map, D-6.)

Brothers Chuck and Paul Hope and their wives Marlyn and Janet have been growing grapes in San Luis Obispo County since 1978. In 1989 they founded their winery, and the best ten percent of their crop now goes into the 3800 cases of Hope Farms Chardonnay, Cabernet Sauvignon, Muscat Canelli, Zinfandel and white Zinfandel produced each year. Picnicking in the gazebo and garden is encouraged and deli items are sold in the tasting room.

JUSTIN VINEYARDS AND WINERY

7 mi off Nacimiento Lake Dr (County Hwy G14) at 11680 Chimney Rock Road, Paso Robles 93446. (805) 238-6932. Open for tasting weekdays 11 am to 5 pm, to 6 pm on weekends. Tours by appointment. (See ACSC *San Luis Obispo County* map, C-4.)

Justin Baldwin purchased 160 acres in the Adelaida Valley in 1982, far off the beaten track of most Paso Robles wineries, and he set about creating a winery that would reward visitors for their long drive. About 8200 cases per year of Cabernet Sauvignon, Cabernet Franc, Chardonnay, Merlot, and a Meritage blend are made, all estate grown, produced, and bottled. The winery also produces a non-alcoholic sorbet from Cabernet Sauvignon grape juice. Visitors are welcome to picnic in the formal English gardens adjacent to the winery.

MARTIN BROTHERS WINERY

1 mi E of Paso Robles off SR 46 (PO Box 2599) at 3610 Buena Vista Dr, Paso Robles 93447. (805) 238-2520. Open daily 11 am to 5 pm for tasting. Tours by appointment only. (See ACSC *San Luis Obispo County* map, C-6.)

The Martin family renovated a degenerating dairy farm in 1981 by building a winery. Besides Chardonnay, Cabernet Sauvignon, Sauvignon Blanc and Zinfandel, they vinify wines from classic Italian varieties, many of them uncommon in California: Aleatico, Nebbiolo, Dolcetto and Sangiovese, among others. They currently own 83 acres of estate vineyards in the Paso Robles area. There are picnic facilities available, and summer concerts are given in the outdoor amphitheater from April to October.

Wineries Open For Tasting Only

The following wineries in the Paso Robles area have tasting rooms on their premises but do not offer tours.

MERIDIAN VINEYARDS

6 mi E of Paso Robles at 7000 Hwy 46 (PO Box 3289), Paso Robles 93447. (805) 237-6000. Open Wed through Mon 10 am to 5 pm; picnic facilities available. (See ACSC *San Luis Obispo County* map, C-7.)

TWIN HILLS WINERY

at jct of Nacimiento Dr and Mustard Creek Rd at 2025 Nacimiento Lake Dr, Paso Robles 93446. (805) 238-9148. Open daily 11 am to 5 pm summer, weekdays noon to 4 pm and weekends 11 am to 5 pm rest of year. Picnic facilities. (See ACSC *San Luis Obispo County* map, C-6.)

SAN MIGUEL

MISSION VIEW VINEYARDS AND WINERY

PO Box 129, San Miguel 93451. (805) 467-3104. Tasting room at US 101 and Wellsona Rd, 3 mi N of Paso Robles. Tasting room open daily 10 am to 6 pm summer, to 6 pm rest of year. Tours and tasting at winery by appointment. (See ACSC *San Luis Obispo County* map, B-6.)

The winery near Mission San Miguel Arcangel produces only 4000 cases per year of Sauvignon, Chardonnay, Sauvignon Blanc and Zinfandel. The vineyards were planted between 1981 and 1983, and the first wine was released in 1984. The grounds are attractively landscaped, and there is a small patio for picnicking. There is also a picnic area at the tasting room at US 101 and Wellsona Road.

Monterey to San Francisco Bay Area

Encompassed in the Monterey to San Francisco Bay Area are the wine grape growing districts of Alameda, Monterey, San Benito, San Mateo, Santa Clara and Santa Cruz counties. Much of this region has climatic features similar to those of the Russian River Area. Sunny valleys are cooled by fog and coastal air currents, providing good conditions for premium wine grapes.

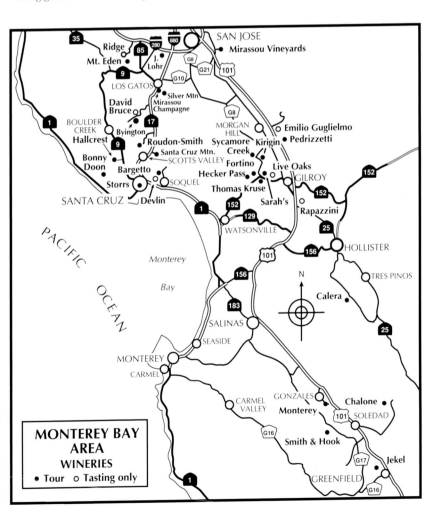

SAN FRANCISCO
BAY AREA
WINERIES
● Tour O Tasting only

To the south, Monterey and San Benito counties have small wineries that are open to the public, but several large wine producers have vineyards in the area. Paul Masson and Mirassou bought acreage between Soledad and Greenfield in 1960. Since then, Almadén and others have followed suit, and vineyards now carpet much of the central and southern Salinas Valley.

Nearby is Northern California's oldest wine district, the Santa Clara Valley. Here the Franciscans planted vineyards at Mission Santa Clara de Asis in 1777, nearly one half century before they introduced wine growing to Sonoma. In recent years, Santa Clara vineyards have been threatened by smog and urban sprawl, forcing many valley wineries to look elsewhere for land.

Another old viticultural area is Santa Cruz County, which supported nearly 40 wineries before Prohibition. As interest in this region has revived, many of the old wineries have been reopened by new owners, and others have been newly constructed. Most of these are small family enterprises, taking advantage of the mountain terrain and coastal climate to make high-quality wines.

On the San Francisco peninsula, the hills of San Mateo County harbor several small wineries, a few of which are open to the public. Although the weather is favorable for premium grapes, high land values preclude the development of large commercial vineyards.

In Alameda County, the gravelly soil of the Livermore Valley is best suited to white wine grapes, although red varieties fare well too. Petite Sirah was pioneered here by Concannon, one of the area's most familiar names. Another well-known Livermore winery is Wente Bros., whose reputation rests largely on white varietal wines.

ANNUAL EVENTS

Exact dates, prices and other information about the events listed below may be verified by calling the telephone numbers shown. Some wineries also individually sponsor open houses, special brunches, dinners and summer concerts. Those interested in the events sponsored by a particular winery should call that winery and ask if a calendar of events is available.

APRIL—

Santa Clara Winegrowers Spring Wine Festival Gilroy. (408) 778-1555, (800) 342-3050. $25 ticket includes barbecue steak dinner, music and wine tasting at this event held at Casa de Fruta. No children.

MAY—

Bluegrass Arts and Wine Festival Felton at Hallcrest Vineyards. (408) 335-4441. Several live bands and arts and crafts booths. Call for ticket information.

"Days of Wine & Rhodies" Santa Cruz at Roudon Smith Vineyards in association with Haver's Rhododendron Nursery. (408) 438-1244. The two businesses lie across the street from one another; the $5 admission includes a tour, a commemorative glass, wine tasting, hors d'oeuvres and live musical entertainment.

Morgan Hill Mushroom Mardi Gras Morgan Hill. (408) 779-9444. Food, arts and crafts booths, wine tent, three stages with continuous entertainment, children's area with games, rides and shows. $6 admission fee.

JUNE—

Epicurean Fare San Jose at Mirassou Vineyards (408) 274-4000. More than 20 Bay Area restaurants participate in this food and wine fair, tasting a variety of items at booths set up in the outdoor courtyard. The $25 tickets go on sale in April and must be ordered in advance. Call the above number and ask for the special events coordinator.

Vintners' Festival various locations throughout San Mateo and Santa Clara counties. (408) 479-9463 (479-WINE). Members of the Santa Cruz Mountains Winegrowers Association open their wineries (some not usually open to the public) during two "passport weekends." For $10, visitors get a commemorative glass that serves as a ticket to each participating winery, which celebrates in its own way. Events include vertical and library tastings, special vintages, art shows, cooking demos and music. For more information, call the association at the number above or write them at P. O. Box 3000, Santa Cruz, 95063.

JULY—

American Pops Concert *San Jose* at Mirassou Vineyards (408) 274-4000. Concert featuring a 60-piece orchestra and fireworks display. Tickets cost $24 and go on sale in May. Call the winery's special events coordinator at the number above.

Fremont Festival of the Arts *Fremont.* (415) 657-1355. Food, arts and crafts booths, two stages with continuous live entertainment, puppet shows, northern California wineries and microbreweries.

AUGUST—

Harvest BBQ *Morgan Hill* at Guglielmo Winery. (408) 779-2145. Family-oriented event with steak barbecue, games and raffles. Call winery to purchase the $25 tickets.

Winery Open House *Alameda* at Rosenblum Cellars. (510) 865-7007.

SEPTEMBER—

Santa Clara Art & Wine Festival *Santa Clara.* (408) 984-3257. Crafts, food and wine booths, live entertainment, children's area with crafts and games. Held at Central Park, 969 Kiely Boulevard.

Capitola Art & Wine Festival *Capitola.* (408) 475-6522. Local wineries, restaurants, crafts and fine arts displays and demonstrations. Live entertainment includes bluegrass, jazz, swing, folk and classical music, theater and dance groups. Children's area has food, entertainment, and participatory art booths designed especially for children. Admission is free; wine tasting $5 for commemorative glass and $1 per tasting ticket.

NOVEMBER—

Holiday Festival *San Jose* at Mirassou Vineyards (408) 274-4000. Festival with strolling carolers, jazz musicians, barbershop quartet, hot-mulled wine. $7 admission includes a commemorative glass.

Winery Open House *Alameda* at Rosenblum Cellars. (510) 865-7007.

DECEMBER—

Christmas Gift Fair *Morgan Hill* at Guglielmo Winery. (408) 779-2145. Boutique gift packs made especially for the holidays are sold. Champagne, cheese and crackers on hand.

Winery Open House *Soledad* at Smith & Hook. (408) 678-2132. All wines are poured for tasting; cheeses and wine cakes available along with holiday gifts.

MONTEREY AND SAN BENITO COUNTIES

GREENFIELD

JEKEL VINEYARDS 1 mi W of US 101 at 40155 Walnut Av (PO Box 336), Greenfield 93927. (408) 674-5525. Open daily 10 am to 5 pm for tasting. Tours by appointment only.

The Jekel family planted 140 acres of vineyards in 1972 and an additional 190 acres a decade later in the Arroyo Seco district of the Salinas Valley. Now owned by Brown-Forman, the ultramodern winery produces 60,000 cases of premium varietals each year; the wines are made from grapes grown in the winery's vineyards, which are planted to Cabernet Franc, Cabernet Sauvignon, Chardonnay, Pinot Noir and Riesling.

SOLEDAD

CHALONE VINEYARD 9 mi E of Soledad off Stonewall Canyon Rd (PO Box 855), Soledad 93960. (408) 678-

1717. Open weekends 11:30 am to 4 pm for tasting and tours. Open weekdays by appointment.

At an elevation of 2000 feet in the Gavilan Mountains, Chalone's location makes viticulture a challenge. The property has been planted to grapes since 1916, although serious winemaking did not begin until the 1960s. Then founder and enologist Richard Graff began to establish Chalone's prestigious reputation for premium wines vinified in the Burgundian style. Winemaker Michael Michaud oversees production of five table wines. Because the vineyard yield is low, annual production rarely exceeds 20,000 cases.

SMITH & HOOK 4 mi N of Soledad off US 101 via Arroyo Seco Rd at 37700 Foothill Rd (PO Drawer C), Soledad 93960. Open daily 11 am to 4 pm for tasting and tours. (408) 678-2132. (See CSAA *Monterey and San Benito Counties* map, F-5.)

The winery and vineyards at Smith & Hook are perched high above the Salinas Valley on the steep eastern slope of the Santa Lucia Mountains. From 250 acres of estate vineyards comes the fruit for 25,000 cases per year of Cabernet Sauvignon. Cabernet has been the winery's specialty since its first vintage in 1979, and winemaker Duane DeBoer has been with the winery since before the vineyard was planted. The winery is housed in a refurbished ranch stable, and guests are welcome to use the picnic area.

Gonzales

THE MONTEREY VINEYARD In Gonzales W of US 101 at 800 S Alta St (PO Box 780), Gonzales 93901. (408) 675-2316. Open daily 10 am to 5 pm for tasting and tours; closed major holidays. (See CSAA *Monterey and San Benito Counties* map, D-6.)

The Monterey Vineyard winery is housed in a large earth-tone stucco building graced by ornamental ironwork and 25-foot stained glass windows. The winery produces five varietal wines from grapes grown in California's coastal counties. Guided tours cover the crushing area and aging cellars. An art gallery houses a permanent exhibit of Ansel Adams photos, commissioned in the early 1960s, that demonstrate the making of wine from bud to glass. There is also a changing exhibit of contemporary California photography. There is a gift shop, picnic facilities and refrigerated deli items.

Hollister

CALERA WINE CO. 11 mi S of Hollister at 11300 Cienega Rd, Hollister 95023. (408) 637-9170. Open by appointment only for tours and sales (no tasting). (See CSAA *Monterey and San Benito Counties* map, D-6.)

Josh Jensen's search for limestone-rich soil ended here—on the site of an abandoned limestone quarry. Having found land similar to that of the Burgundian vineyards he worked in and loved, he began searching for the wine that would satisfy him as well. Construction began in 1977 on Calera's gravity-flow winery, which spans six levels on a hillside in the Gavilan Mountains. Calera's six vineyards all lie within the Mount Harlan appellation defined in 1990. The winery makes three varietals: Chardonnay, Pinot Noir and tiny amounts of Viognier.

SANTA CRUZ COUNTY

BARGETTO WINERY 3535 N Main St, Soquel 95073. (408) 475-2258. Open daily 9 am to 5 pm for tasting.

Tours weekdays by appointment at 11 am and 2 pm. (See CSAA *Santa Cruz and Vicinity* map, H-10.) A tasting room is also located at 700 Cannery Row, Monterey; (408) 373-4053. Open 10 am to 6 pm daily.

The Bargettos established their coastal winery in 1933, and it still remains a family operation. Housed in a brown barn on Soquel Creek, the winery produces a selection of fruit and table wines, including mead. The Bargetto wines are served in the rustic tasting room and on the outdoor patio overlooking the creek, and there is a gift shop and refrigerated deli items.

BONNY DOON VINEYARD 12 mi N of Santa Cruz via SR 1 and Bonny Doon Rd at 10 Pine Flat Rd (PO Box 8376), Santa Cruz 95061. (408) 425-3625. Open for tasting daily except Tue, noon to 5 pm, May 15 through Sep 14; noon to 5 pm Thu through Mon rest of year. Closed major holidays. Tours by appointment. (See CSAA *Peninsula Points* map.)

Philosophy major turned viticulturalist/winemaker Randall Grahm opened his small winery in a bucolic setting four miles from the ocean in the Santa Cruz Mountains in 1983. Concentrating on wines made from the prominent grape varieties of France's Rhone and Provence regions and on Italian varieties, Bonny Doon currently produces premium varietal wines and eclectic blends from estate-grown and purchased fruit. Visitors are welcome to picnic under the redwoods.

BYINGTON WINERY & VINE-YARDS, INC. 5.5 mi up Bear Creek Rd off SR 17 at 21850 Bear Creek Rd, Los Gatos 95030. (408) 354-1111 ext. 204. Open daily 11 am to 5 pm for tasting. Tours by appointment.

Off winding Bear Creek Road, Byington's majestic Italian-style chateau rises out of the redwoods and vineyards of the Santa Cruz Mountains. Winemaker Greg Bruni, whose family owned San Martin Winery, vinifies Sauvignon Blanc, Chardonnay, Johannisberg Riesling, Cabernet Sauvignon, Pinot Noir, Merlot and Zinfandel from estate and purchased fruit. Annual production of 10,000 cases is distributed through the tasting room and mail order. Visitors who wish to tour the winery or use the barbecues and picnic tables should call ahead. The 2000-foot elevation provides a spectacular view of the Monterey Bay.

HALLCREST VINEYARDS 6 mi N of Santa Cruz at 379 Felton-Empire Rd, Felton 95018. (408) 335-4441. Open daily 11 am to 5:30 pm for tasting. Tours by appointment only. (See CSAA *Peninsula Points* map.)

Hallcrest Vineyards were founded in 1941 by Chafee Hall, and the last Hallcrest label vintage was pressed in 1964, when Hall retired. Several wineries maintained the vineyards after his death in 1968 until Felton-Empire Vineyards reopened the site in the late 1970s. In 1987, the Schumacher family bought the property and restored its original name. Now, Hallcrest produces about 15,000 cases per year of a large number of varietal wines and varietal grape juices. The winery is also the second largest producer of organic wines in the United States and uses the Organic Wine Works label for its organic wines. A picturesque picnic area overlooks the vineyards.

ROUDON-SMITH VINEYARDS 2 mi N of Scotts Valley Dr at 2364 Bean Creek Rd, Santa Cruz 95066. (408) 438-1244. Open weekends 10:30 am to 4:30 pm by appointment for tasting and tours (call for directions). (See CSAA *Santa Cruz and Vicinity* map, B-5.)

A pair of former engineers made the first Roudon-Smith wines in the Santa Cruz Mountains in 1972. The winery moved to its present rustic location in 1978, and production is now 10,000 cases per year. Attention is focused on a few premium varietals, with an emphasis on Santa Cruz Mountains Estate Chardonnay, and on Cabernet Sauvignon, Petite Sirah and Zinfandel vinified from grapes grown in various California coastal regions.

SANTA CRUZ MOUNTAIN VINEYARD 2300 Jarvis Rd, Santa Cruz 95065. (408) 426-6209. Open by appointment only for tasting and tours. (See CSAA *Santa Cruz and Vicinity* map, A-9.)

Ken Burnap founded his winery in 1974, and has since expanded his original Pinot Noir production to include Chardonnay, Merlot and Cabernet Sauvignon. The four varietals account for the compact winery's total output of 3000 cases per year. Traditional methods are used to vinify grapes grown in unirrigated mountain vineyards. Visitors with appointments follow a narrow, scenic mountain road to the winery.

SILVER MOUNTAIN VINE-YARDS at PO Box 3636, Santa Cruz 95063. (408) 353-2278. Open by appointment.

Jerold O'Brien, a retired military pilot, embraced the myriad difficulties of mountain vineyard farming here in the Santa Cruz Mountains. Founded in 1979, the original winery and cellar were destroyed in the 1989 Loma Prieta earthquake, but O'Brien saw it as an opportunity to start over and create better facilities. Production, which dropped after the earthquake, is only about 1700 cases per year. Ten acres of vineyards lie adjacent to the winery. Visitors who call for an appointment and directions to

the winery will receive a tour, which may include tasting. O'Brien makes Chardonnay, Zinfandel and Cabernet Sauvignon in a French Bordeaux style, plus an Italian-style Zinfandel. The winery holds a sunset tasting series in the spring and a fireside tasting series in the fall, both of which require reservations.

STORRS WINERY .5 mi S of Hwy 1 off River Street exit at Old Sash Mill, 303 Potrero St, Santa Cruz 95060. (408) 458-5030. Open for tasting and tours daily except Wed, noon to 5 pm, Apr 15 to Oct 15; noon to 5 pm Fri through Mon rest of year. (See CSAA *Santa Cruz and Vicinity* map, J-5).

Stephen and Pamela Storrs founded Storrs Winery in 1988, and their winery is one of only a handful operated by a husband and wife enology team. They vinify Chardonnay, Gewürztraminer and Zinfandel from Santa Cruz Mountain grapes, and Merlot from San Ysidro grapes. Their selection of low-tonnage, coastal-area vines produces only enough fruit for about 4000 cases per year.

Winery Open For Tasting Only
The following winery has a tasting room on the premises but does not offer tours.

DEVLIN WINE CELLARS 1 mi N of SR-1 at 3801 Park Av, Soquel 95073. (408) 476-7288. Open weekends noon to 5 pm. (See CSAA *Santa Cruz* map, G-11.)

SANTA CLARA COUNTY

GILROY

FORTINO WINERY 5 mi W of Gilroy at 4525 Hecker Pass Hwy, Gilroy 95020. (408) 842-3305 and (408) 847-0387. Open daily 9 am to 6 pm for tasting and tours; closed major holidays. Deli open daily 9 am to 5 pm. (See CSAA *Peninsula Points* map.)

In 1970 Ernest Fortino purchased the Cassa Brothers' winery and began converting production from bulk to varietal wines. The owner may lead the tasting, and guided tours include everything from vineyards to bottling line. There is a picnic area, gift shop and European boutique.

HECKER PASS WINERY 5 mi W of Gilroy at 4605 Hecker Pass Hwy, Gilroy 95020. (408) 842-8755. Open daily for tasting and tours, May through Sep, 10 am to 6 pm; 10 am to 5 pm rest of year. (See CSAA *Peninsula Points* map.)

The equipment at this 21-year-old enterprise reflects a mixture of winemaking techniques: old basket presses and redwood tanks share room with oak barrels and jacketed stainless-steel tanks. The Hecker Pass label appears on a selection of dry table wines, as well as sherries and ports. Visitors may sample the wines at one of the two 20-foot redwood bars in the tasting room, and they are welcome to use the picnic area.

KIRIGIN CELLARS 5 mi W of Gilroy via SR 152 and Co Rd G8 at 11550 Watsonville Rd, Gilroy 95020. (408) 847-8827. Open daily for tasting, 10 am to 6 pm summer, to 5 pm rest of year. Tours by appointment only. (See CSAA *Peninsula Points* map.)

Nikola Kirigin-Chargin acquired this winery in 1976. Stainless-steel tanks add a modern touch to the venerable building, which dates back to 1827.

THOMAS KRUSE WINERY 5 mi W of Gilroy at 4390 Hecker Pass Hwy, Gilroy 95020. (408) 842-7016. Open daily noon to 5 pm for tasting and

tours;closed major holidays. (See CSAA *Peninsula Points* map.)

In 1971 Tom Kruse launched his two-man operation, one of the smallest wineries in Santa Clara County. The vineyards cover only one acre, and because of space limitations, Kruse prefers to limit tour groups to five people. The wine list includes a number of dry varietal table wines, plus two bottle-fermented sparkling wines. In addition to personally explaining his winemaking operations, Kruse often hosts the wine tasting.

SARAH'S VINEYARD 5 mi W of Gilroy at 4005 Hecker Pass Hwy, Gilroy 95020. (408) 842-4278. Tasting and tours by appointment only. (See CSAA *Peninsula Points* map.)

This small winery is located in a shaded redwood building on a hillside overlooking a 10-acre Chardonnay vineyard, an apple orchard and rolling hills. Here, winemaker Marilyn Otteman produces about 2000 cases annually of Chardonnay and red table wine from estate grapes and from grapes purchased from selected growers.

Wineries Open For Tasting Only

The following wineries in Gilroy have tasting rooms on the premises but do not offer tours.

LIVE OAKS WINERY 4 mi W of Gilroy at 3875 Hecker Pass Hwy, Gilroy 95020. (408) 842-2401. Open daily 10 am to 5 pm; closed New Year's Day, Easter, Thanksgiving and Christmas. Picnic area. (See CSAA *Peninsula Points* map.)

RAPAZZINI WINERY 3 mi S of Gilroy on US 101 (PO Box 247), Gilroy 95020. (408) 842-5649. Open daily 9 am to 6 pm in summer; weekdays 9 am to 5 pm and weekends 9 am to 6 pm rest of year. Next door to the winery is the Garlic Shoppe, which also has a tasting bar in addition to gift and gourmet items (408) 848-3646. (See CSAA *Peninsula Points* map.)

MORGAN HILL

PEDRIZZETTI WINERY 1 mi E of Morgan Hill off US 101 via Dunne and Murphy Avs at 1645 San Pedro Av, Morgan Hill 95037. (408) 779-7389. Open daily 10 am to 5 pm for tasting; tours by appointment only. (See CSAA *Peninsula Points* map.)

The Pedrizzettis bought their winery in 1945. Their enterprise has been based on table wines, notably Petite Sirah and white Zinfandel. In addition, the list includes dessert, aperitif and sparkling varieties. Visitors are welcome to picnic, and Phyllis Pedrizzetti guides visitors with appointments on a tour of the winery.

Winery Open For Tasting Only

The following winery in Morgan Hill has tasting rooms on the premises but do not offer tours.

EMILIO GUGLIELMO WINERY 1480 E Main Av, Morgan Hill 95037. (408) 779-2145. Open weekdays 9 am to 5 pm, weekends 10 am to 5 pm; closed holidays. (See CSAA *Peninsula Points* map.)

SAN JOSE

J. LOHR WINERY 1000 Lenzen Ave, San Jose 95126. (408) 288-5057. Open daily 10 am to 5 pm for tasting. Tours weekends at 11 am and 2 pm. (See CSAA *San Jose-Northern Area* map, N-15.)

Jerry Lohr's winery released its first wines in 1974. Estate-owned vineyards are located in Monterey County, the Napa Valley and Paso Robles.

Production is about 250,000 cases annually, and current offerings include Cabernet Sauvignon, Chardonnay, Gamay, Johannisberg Riesling, Merlot, Sauvignon Blanc and white Zinfandel.

MIRASSOU VINEYARDS In San Jose 1.5 mi E of Capitol Expy at 3000 Aborn Rd, San Jose 95135. (408) 274-4000. Open Mon through Sat 10 am to 5 pm, Sun noon to 4 pm for tasting and tours. (See CSAA *Peninsula Points* map.)

Mirassou family tradition holds that when Pierre Pellier ran out of water for his vine cuttings on the ship from Europe to America, he bought a shipment of potatoes on board and planted his cuttings in them for moisture. He built his winery in 1860, six years after planting his first vineyards, and in 1881 his oldest daughter married Pierre Mirassou. Now in its fifth generation of family ownership with brothers Daniel, Jim and Peter, Mirassou produces a number of vintage-dated varietal wines at its San Jose facility. Special events and programs are held throughout the year.

LOS GATOS

MIRASSOU CHAMPAGNE CELLARS .5 mi off Main St at 300 College Av, Los Gatos 95032. (408) 395-3790. Open daily noon to 5 pm for tasting and tours. (See CSAA *San Jose-Central Area* map, O-2.)

The fourth generation of Mirassous, Edmund and Norbert, produced Mirassou's first bottling of méthode champenoise sparkling wine in 1954 to celebrate the 100th anniversary of family winemaking. Today, the sparkling wines are made at the old Novitiate Winery in the foothills above Los Gatos, where the Jesuits produced wines from 1888 to 1985. From vineyards to bottling line, tours take in the entire operation, and an assortment of table and sparkling wines is offered in the tasting room.

Winery Open For Tasting Only

The following winery in Los Gatos has a tasting room on the premises but does not offer tours.

DAVID BRUCE WINERY 5 mi SW of Los Gatos at 21439 Bear Creek Rd, Los Gatos 95030. (408) 354-4214. Open Wed through Sun noon to 5 pm. Picnic area. (See CSAA *Peninsula Points* map.)

SARATOGA
MOUNT EDEN VINEYARDS

22020 Mt Eden Rd, Saratoga 95070. (408) 867-5832. Tasting and tours by appointment. (See CSAA *Peninsula Points* map.)

Mount Eden is a small winery located at an elevation of 2000 feet in the Santa Cruz Mountains. From vines first planted by Martin Ray in the 1940s and from non-estate Chardonnay grapes purchased from the MacGregor Vineyards in Edna Valley, the winery produces a few thousand cases of Chardonnay, Cabernet Sauvignon and Pinot Noir. In 1991, construction was completed on a 4000-square-foot cave. Arrangements to visit the winery should be made at least a week ahead.

CUPERTINO
Winery Open For Tasting Only

The following winery in Cupertino has a tasting room on the premises but does not offer tours.

RIDGE VINEYARDS 7 mi NW of SR-280 via Foothill Bl/Stevens Cyn Rd at 17100 Monte Bello Rd, Cupertino 95014. (408) 867-3233.

Open Sat and Sun 11 am to 3 pm. (See CSAA *Peninsula Points* map.)

EASTERN SAN FRANCISCO BAY AREA

CEDAR MOUNTAIN WINERY 4 mi SE of downtown Livermore at 7000 Tesla Rd, Livermore 94550. (510) 373-6636 or 449-9215. Open weekends and holidays noon to 4 p.m. or by appointment for tasting and tours.

Linda and Earl Ault purchased a four-year-old Chenin Blanc vineyard in 1988, dubbed it Blanches Vineyard and the next year grafted it to Chardonnay and Cabernet Sauvignon. They now produce about 1500 cases per year from their small but growing facility, named after Cedar Mountain Ridge just south of the winery. The works of local artists (including Ault's) are displayed in the tasting room, and picnic facilities are available.

CONCANNON VINEYARD 2 mi SE of Livermore at 4590 Tesla Rd (County Rd J2), Livermore 94550. (510) 447-3760. Open weekdays 10 am to 4:30 pm, weekends 11 am to 4:30 pm for tasting and tours. (See CSAA *Bay and River Area* map.)

James Concannon left his native Ireland for America at age 18 in 1865 and established his Livermore vineyard 28 years later. In 1992, it was sold to Tesla Vineyards (part-owned by Wente). Today, Cabernet Sauvignon, Petite Sirah (which Concannon Vineyard pioneered as a new varietal in 1964), Chardonnay and Sauvignon Blanc are produced from the yields of the surrounding vineyards. Visitors are invited to sample the wines, picnics and tour the winery, and horse carriage tours of the vineyard are offered weekends from noon to 3 pm and weekdays by appointment.

LIVERMORE VALLEY CELLARS 1 mi S of Livermore off SR 84 at 1508 Wetmore Rd, Livermore 94550. (510) 447-1751. Open daily 11:30 am to 5 pm for tasting and tours. (See CSAA *Bay and River Area* map.)

This small winery, built in 1978, is located in an insulated metal building seemingly on the verge of being overwhelmed by suburban housing tracts. The Lagiss family produces wine from grapes from their 34-acre vineyard, which is planted to Grey Riesling, Chardonnay, Golden Chasselas, French Colombard and Servant Blanc. The yield ranges from 1000 to 3000 cases per year, with fruit purchased from other vineyards during drought years. There are picnic facilities and a park nearby.

MURRIETA'S WELL .25 mi S of jct of Tesla and Mines rds at 3005 Mines Rd, Livemore 94550. (510) 449-9229. Open weekdays by appointment for tasting and tours, weekends 11 am to 4:30 pm; $5 tasting fee.

Murrieta's Well is named after the watering site (which lies on the property) often used by legendary outlaw Joaquin Murrieta. A joint venture between Sergio Traverso and Philip Wente, the winery calls up images both of the romance of wine and the heyday of the ranchos. Restoration of the 1890s structure, which opened to the public in December 1992, began in the 1980s. Antique winemaking equipment and old photographs line the upstairs walls, and sit-down tastings are done at tables made from old barrels topped with glass. Winemaker Traverso focuses his efforts on two proprietary blends (currently the winery's only national releases), and two

styles of Chardonnay and a Zinfandel which are available only at the winery.

RETZLAFF VINEYARDS 2 mi S of downtown Livermore at 1356 South Livermore Av, Livermore 94550. (510) 447-8941. Open weekdays noon to 2 pm, weekends noon to 5 pm; $3 tasting fee refundable with purchase.

In a green barn behind an 1885 farmhouse, Bob and Gloria Taylor vinify Cabernet Sauvignon, Chardonnay, Grey Riesling, Merlot, Sauvignon Blanc and a Meritage blend from their 14 acres of vineyards. The former sheep ranch was planted to grapes in 1977, the first vintage was crushed in 1986, and annual production now stands at 3000 cases per year. Retzlaff Vineyards is the closest winery to downtown Livermore, and the expansive shaded picnic area is a popular lunchtime destination for tourists and businesspersons alike. The winery also hosts a series of "Full Moon Dinners" from late spring to early autumn.

ROSENBLUM CELLARS opposite the Alameda Naval Air Station at 2900 Main St, Alameda 94501. (510) 865-7007. Open weekends 10 am to 5 pm for tasting and tours, and on weekdays by appointment. (See CSAA *Oakland-Berkeley-Alameda* map, K-2.)

California's only island winery is housed in a spacious former locomotive repair barn in Alameda. Winemaker Kent Rosenblum purchases grapes from older and hillside dry-farmed vineyards in Napa and Sonoma counties. The winery specializes in Zinfandel, Cabernet Sauvignon, Merlot and Petite Sirah, and it produces small quantities of white varietal wines and a méthode champenoise sparkling Gewürztraminer. Visitors will get a crash course in Rosenblum's traditional yet innovative production techniques.

STONY RIDGE WINERY 2.5 mi SE of downtown Livermore at 4948 Tesla Rd, Livermore 94550. (510) 449-0458. Open for tasting Mon through Sat 11 am to 5 pm, Sun noon to 5 pm. Restaurant open Mon through Sat 11 am to 2 pm. Tours by appointment.

Carrying a deep appreciation for the history of the Livermore Valley and for her own family history, Monica Scotto bought the Stony Ridge Winery brand in 1985 and, along with her family, began working to restore the brand's former prestige. Annual production consists of 20,000 cases per year of seven varietal and two blended wines, all available for tasting. The tasting bar, once part of their father's Pleasanton winery, runs along one side of the tasting room, which shares space with the Scotto's restaurant. A large redwood deck fronts the structure and provides a place for outdoor dining in the summer.

WEIBEL VINEYARDS 1 mi S of Mission San Jose via SR 238 at 1250 Stanford Av (PO Box 3398), Mission San Jose 94539. (510) 656-2340. Open daily 10 am to 5 pm for tasting and until 3 pm for tours. (See CSAA *Fremont-Newark* map, H-14.)

The Weibel vineyards were originally the domain of Leland Stanford, who founded his winery in 1869. The winery has been named a historical landmark and since 1945 has been owned by the Weibel family, which also owns property in Mendocino County's Redwood Valley. Ten-minute guided tours are offered from 10 a.m. to 3 p.m. Monday through Friday. There is a tasting room set amidst a grove of trees, with a picnic area adjacent.

WENTE BROS. ESTATE WINERY 2 mi SE of Livermore at 5565 Tesla Rd, Livermore 94550. (510) 447-3603. Open Mon through Sat 10 am to 4:30 pm, Sun 11 am to 4:30 pm for tasting. Tours offered Mon through Sat 10 and 11 am and 1, 2 and 3 pm; Sun at 1, 2 and 3 pm. (See CSAA *Bay and River Area* map.)

The fourth generation of Wentes now oversees the winery Carl Wente launched in 1883. Production is centered in the Livermore Valley, where guides give a thorough tour of the facility. Tours and tasting are also available at nearby Wente Bros. Sparkling Wine Cellars, situated in a restored old winery with deep sandstone caves for bottle aging. The Sparkling Wine Cellars are located at 5050 Arroyo Rd, (510) 447-3694. Hours and tour schedule are the same as those of the Estate Winery. Each location sometimes hosts private events; visitors are advised to call ahead before visiting.

Wineries Open For Tasting Only

The following wineries have tasting rooms on the premises but do not offer tours.

CADENASSO WINERY 4144 Abernathy Rd, Suisun 94585. (707) 425-5845. Open daily 9 am to 5:30 pm.

FENESTRA WINERY 1 mi W of jct of SR 84 and Holmes St/Wetmore Rd at 83 E Vallecitos Rd, Livermore 94550. (510) 447-5246. Open weekends noon to 5 pm for tasting. Picnic facilities.

WESTERN SAN FRANCISCO BAY AREA

PAGE MILL WINERY 13686 Page Mill Rd, Los Altos Hills 94022. (415) 948-0958. Open by appointment only for tasting and tours. (See CSAA *Palo Alto* map, L-8.)

Dick Stark's basement winery saw its first crush of 1000 gallons in 1976. With his whole family assisting, production had tripled the next year and has now leveled off at 2500 cases annually. Four varietal table wines are made from purchased grapes. Because the winery is part of the Stark residence, appointments to visit the winery are essential.

WOODSIDE VINEYARDS 340 Kings Mountain Rd, Woodside 94062-3618. (415) 851-3144. Open weekends by appointment only for tasting and tours. (See CSAA *Palo Alto* map, H-2.)

Woodside Vineyards was founded in 1960, when the owners built a wine cellar under their carport. The grapes are grown on 15 acres from gnarled stock of the old La Questa vineyards, abandoned long ago. Woodside wines, which include Cabernet Sauvignon, Pinot Noir, Zinfandel and Chardonnay, are available in extremely limited quantities.

Winery Open for Tasting Only

The following winery in Half Moon Bay has a tasting room on the premises but does not offer tours.

OBESTER WINERY 2 mi E of Half Moon Bay at 12341 San Mateo Rd (SR 92), Half Moon Bay 94019. (415) 726-9463. Open daily 10 am to 5 pm. (See CSAA *San Mateo* map, J-7.) A second winery is located in the Anderson Valley (see listing under Philo in Mendocino County).

Mendocino, Lake and Northern Sonoma Counties

Stretching through Sonoma and Mendocino counties, the Russian River passes between ridges of the Coast Range. This area, with climate zones similar to the Napa Valley's, has been producing wine for over a century. Wineries are scattered along most of the river's length, which parallels US 101 from Redwood Valley to Healdsburg and then heads west to the Pacific. More wineries are located in tributary valleys and in the Anderson Valley, a separate region enjoying a mild climate and high rainfall.

For many years most of the area's grapes went into bulk and jug wines, but the 1960s brought increasing interest in the potential for producing premium wines. Most wineries in the area responded to the trend and began concentrating their efforts on vintage-dated varietals.

The wine boom brought numerous newcomers to the Russian River, Dry Creek, Alexander, Redwood and Anderson valleys. Among them are many small wineries that devote their attention to a limited, select stock of premium varietal wines.

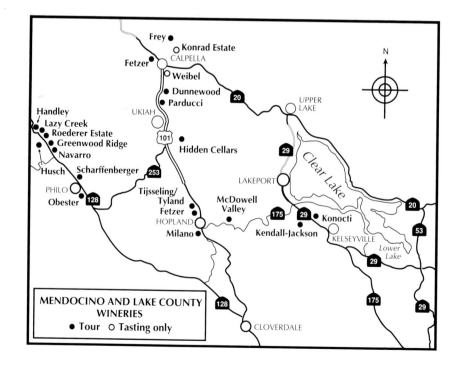

Michelle De Lude

The Russian River winds through Mendocino and Sonoma counties to the Pacific Ocean and helps define the Alexander, Dry Creek and Russian River valley appellations.

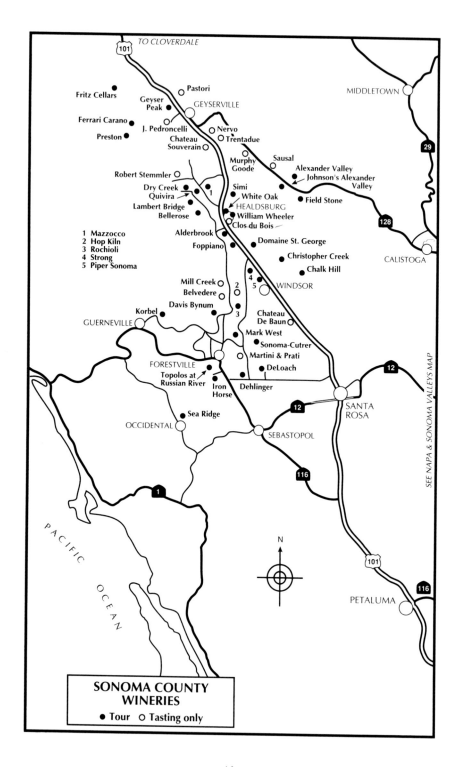

TO CLOVERDALE

101

MIDDLETOWN

Fritz Cellars

Pastori

Geyser Peak

GEYSERVILLE

Ferrari Carano

J. Pedroncelli

Preston

Nervo

Trentadue

Chateau Souverain

29

Murphy Goode

Sausal

Robert Stemmler

Alexander Valley

Johnson's Alexander Valley

Dry Creek

Simi

Quivira

White Oak

Field Stone

Lambert Bridge

HEALDSBURG

Bellerose

William Wheeler

Clos du Bois

128

1 Mazzocco

Alderbrook

2 Hop Kiln

Domaine St. George

3 Rochioli

Foppiano

4 Strong

Christopher Creek

5 Piper Sonoma

Chalk Hill

CALISTOGA

Mill Creek

4

Belvedere

2

5

WINDSOR

Davis Bynum

3

Korbel

Chateau De Baun

GUERNEVILLE

Mark West

Sonoma-Cutrer

12

Martini & Prati

FORESTVILLE

DeLoach

Topolos at Russian River

Iron Horse

Dehlinger

12

SANTA ROSA

Sea Ridge

OCCIDENTAL

SEBASTOPOL

116

PACIFIC OCEAN

N

101

1

116

PETALUMA

SEE NAPA & SONOMA VALLEYS MAP

SONOMA COUNTY WINERIES

● Tour   ○ Tasting only

Operating on a larger scale and for a broader market are a number of very big and impressively constructed facilities. The Sonoma County Wine and Visitors Center, newly opened in Rohnert Park, offers travelers video views of county scenery in addition to wine tasting, a demonstration vineyard, cooking classes, special tours and events, and retail sales of wine and gifts. The center is located at 5000 Roberts Lake Road via Golf Course Drive; telephone (707) 586-3795.

The "Russian River Wine Road," established in 1976, presently links more than 50 wineries in this region that welcome visitors; special directional signs are posted on local roads between Windsor and Cloverdale. For help in locating wineries in this section, refer to the CSAA North Bay Counties map; members can obtain more detailed maps of the area in person at any office of the California State Automobile Association.

ANNUAL EVENTS

Exact dates, prices and other information about the events listed below may be verified by calling the telephone numbers shown. Some wineries also individually sponsor special brunches, dinners and summer concerts. Those interested in the events sponsored by a particular winery should call that winery and ask if a calendar of events is available.

JANUARY—
Winter Wineland *various locations in Sonoma County.* (707) 433-6782; in California, (800) 648-9922. Pick up a flyer and visit participating wineries for food pairings, vertical and library tastings, entertainment and art shows. Purchase of commemorative glass necessary for tasting: $10.

MARCH—
Russian River Wine Road Barrel Tasting *various locations in Sonoma County.* (707) 433-6782; in California, (800) 648-9922. Tasting of "wines in progress," often from the barrel, and "component tasting," in which the different wines used in blending can be tasted separately.

APRIL—
Pick of the Vine *various locations in Sonoma County's Russian River Valley.* (707) 433-6782; in California, (800) 648-9922. The $18 ticket includes a souvenir glass for wine tasting and a carrier plate for sampling food.

MAY—
Russian River Wine Festival *various locations in Sonoma County.* (707) 433-6782; in California, (800) 648-9922. Music, food, crafts, wine tasting in the park; barbecues, formal dinners, special wine events. $15 includes souvenir glass.

Summer Chardonnay Celebration
Cloverdale at J. Fritz Winery. (707) 894-3389. Pre-release tastings of Chardonnay accompany barbecue.

JULY —
California Wine Tasting Championships *Philo* at Greenwood Ridge Vineyards. (707) 895-2002. Wine tasters must be 21 years of age, but families will also find cheese-tasting, chocolate, music and picnicking. Advance registration costs $25 per person or $40 per couple ($30 and $45 at the door).

AUGUST—
Sonoma County Showcase and Wine Auction *various locations and events in Sonoma County.* (707) 579-0577. Many events may be combined or attended separately: a barrel auction, semi-formal dinners, wine tasting, vineyard and winery tours, luncheons and themed events. Call for schedule and prices.

Mendocino Bounty Valley Food and Wine Center, Hopland. (707) 744-1250. Agricultural fair with wineries, nurseries, livestock, and other food producers participating. Wine, beer and specialty food tasting, panel discussions, flower and plant arrangements. $10 tickets must be ordered in advance from Fetzer Vineyard, PO Box 227, Redwood Valley 95470.

SEPTEMBER—

Winesong *Fort Bragg.* (707) 964-5186. This annual benefit celebration costs $55 and includes a tasting, a live and silent auction. More than 100 wineries, 40 restaurants and ten music groups participate.

Mendocino County Fair & Apple Show *Boonville.* (707) 462-6664.

OCTOBER—

Harvest Festival and Warehouse Sale *Kelseyville* at Konocti Winery. (707) 279-4395.

Sonoma County Harvest Fair *Santa Rosa,* at Sonoma County Fairgrounds. (707) 545-4203. Crafts, artwork, wine tasting and judging, food presentations by local restauranteurs.

Crush Festival *Fulton* at Chateau de Baun. (707) 571-7500. Visitors have the opportunity for a hands-on experience. Events include grape picking, winemaking, wine judging, grape stomp competition and barbecue.

NOVEMBER—

Zinful Celebration *Cloverdale* Fritz Cellars. (707) 894-3389. Pre-release and vertical tastings, barbecue.

Holly Days Craft Fair *Fulton* Chateau de Baun. (707) 571-7500. Handmade wreaths, dolls, ornaments, quilts, clothing, jams and herb vinegars are among the crafts offered for sale.

NORTHERN SONOMA COUNTY

SANTA ROSA AREA

Including the cities of Sebastopol, Occidental, Forestville, Fulton and Guerneville

DEHLINGER WINERY 6300 Guerneville Rd, Sebastopol, CA 95472. (707) 823-2378. Open daily 10 am to 5 pm for tasting and tours. (See CSAA *Sonoma and Napa Counties* map, F-7.)

Tom Dehlinger planted 14 acres of premium grape vines in 1975 on his ranch north of Sebastopol. He now produces about 8000 cases per year of Chardonnay, Pinot Noir, Merlot and Cabernet Sauvignon exclusively from his 45-acre vineyard adjacent to the winery. Dehlinger uses traditional winemaking practices aimed at the production of assertively aromatic and flavorful table wines.

DE LOACH VINEYARDS 5 mi W of Santa Rosa at 1791 Olivet Rd, Santa Rosa, CA 95401. (707) 526-9111. Open daily 10 am to 4:30 pm for tasting. Tours weekdays at 2 pm and weekends at 11 am and 2 pm. (See CSAA *Sonoma and Napa Counties* map, E-8.)

DeLoach's redwood winery building stands in the midst of fields of vineyards, some of which date from 1905. The DeLoach family now produces 100,000 cases annually of a large number of premium varietal wines from their 278 acres of grapes grown in the Russian River Valley. Picnic facilities and horseshoe pits lie under the redwood trees adjacent to the winery, and the tasting room displays work by local artists.

Bottling lines can take up hundreds of square feet, or they can fit into the back of a small truck, like this one at Dehlinger.

Michelle De Lude

IRON HORSE VINEYARDS 9786 Ross Station Rd, Sebastopol, CA 95472. (707) 887-1507. Tasting by appointment only, Sat 9 am to 3:30 pm. Tours by appointment weekdays at 10 am and 2 pm (includes tasting). (See CSAA *Sonoma and Napa Counties* map, F-7.)

Founded in 1979, Iron Horse presently produces Cabernet Sauvignon, Chardonnay, Pinot Noir and Sauvignon Blanc table wine and several different sparkling wines. Grapes are grown in the 140-acre home vineyard in the western foothills of Sonoma County and at the winemaker's vineyard in the Alexander Valley. The current production level is 38,000 cases per year.

KORBEL CHAMPAGNE CELLARS 4 mi N of Santa Rosa and 12 mi W of US 101 at 13250 River Rd, Guerneville, CA 95446. (707) 887-2294. Open daily 9 am to 5 pm in summer for tasting; to 4:30 pm rest of year. Tours daily between 10 am and 3:45 pm in summer, noon to 3:45 rest of year. Garden tours are offered during the summer 11 am to 3 pm. (See CSAA *Sonoma and Napa Counties* map, E-6.)

Korbel bears the name of its founders, three brothers who launched the business in the 1870s. Here among the redwoods on the Russian River, the winery and adjoining brandy tower were built as replicas of buildings in the Korbels' native Bohemia. By 1954, when the winery was bought by the Heck family, the Korbel reputation for sparkling wines and brandy was firmly established. In 1993, Korbel's sparkling wine was served at the 1993 Presidential Inaugural events. Tours of the winery include the Korbel history museum, a multi-media presentation on the production of sparkling wine and a walk through the century-old cellars.

MARK WEST VINEYARDS 11 mi NW of Santa Rosa off River Rd at 7000 Trenton-Healdsburg Rd, Forestville, CA 95436. (707) 836-0551. Open daily 10 am to 5 pm for tasting and tours. (See CSAA *Sonoma and Napa Counties* map, E-7.)

Named after a prominent Sonoma pioneer, this winery was founded in 1976 by Robert and Joan Ellis. Now, Mark West is part of the Forestville Wine Group. Chardonnay, Gewürztraminer and Pinot Noir are produced from 66 acres of estate vineyards. Visitors are welcome to picnic; large groups should call ahead.

SEA RIDGE WINERY 1 mi NE of Occidental, PO Box 951, Occidental, CA 95465. (707) 874-1707. Open by appointment only for tasting and tours. (See CSAA *Sonoma and Napa Counties* map, F-7.)

Marine biologist Dan Wickham and his wife, nature educator Dee Wickham, moved their coastal winery inland to the former site of the Lemorel Winery, built by Lee Morelli around the turn of the century. A few photos and displays from their Bodega Bay tasting room have followed them into their new location among the redwoods, where they maintain the old winery as close to its original state as possible. They produce only 1500 cases per year of Chardonnay, Merlot, Pinot Noir and Zinfandel, some from vines nearly as old as the winery.

TOPOLOS AT RUSSIAN RIVER VINEYARDS In Forestville at 5700 Gravenstein Hwy N (SR 116; PO Box 358), Forestville, CA 95436. (707) 887-1575. Open daily 11 am to 5 pm for tasting. Tours by appointment only. Restaurant open daily from Memorial through Labor days, Wed through Sun rest of year; (707) 887-1562. (See CSAA *Sonoma and Napa Counties* map, E-7.)

The winery at Russian River Vineyards is modeled after Sonoma County's hop kilns and the old Russian stockade at Fort Ross. The hybrid structure was built in 1969; the Topolos family took over in 1978 and has expanded the 8000-case-per-year list to include six varietals made from grapes organically grown on the adjacent 25-acre vineyard and from other nearby vineyards. The building also houses a restaurant that serves Continental and Greek cuisine.

Wineries Open For Tasting Only

The following wineries in the Santa Rosa area have tasting rooms on the premises but do not offer tours.

CHATEAU DE BAUN .5 mi N of River Rd at 5007 Fulton Rd (PO Box 11483, Santa Rosa, CA 95406), Fulton, CA 95439. (707) 571-7500. Open daily 10 am to 5 pm. Demonstration vineyard, gift shop, picnic facilities, summer dinner concerts. (See CSAA *Sonoma and Napa Counties* map, E-8.)

MARTINI & PRATI, INC. 7 mi W of Santa Rosa at 2191 Laguna Rd, Santa Rosa, CA 95401. (707) 823-2404. Open daily Mar through Nov, 11 am to 4 pm; Dec and Feb, Fri through Sun, 11 am to 4 pm; closed Jan. (See CSAA *Sonoma and Napa Counties* map, E-7.)

WINDSOR

PIPER SONOMA CELLARS 12 mi N of Santa Rosa at 11447 Old Redwood Hwy, Healdsburg, CA 95448. (707) 433-8843. Open daily 10 am to 4 pm for complimentary tasting, retail sales, wine by the glass and self-guided tours. Guided tours by appointment. (See CSAA *Sonoma and Napa Counties* map, D-7.)

This sparkling wine operation is the California venture of the French champagne firm of Piper-Heidsieck. The first harvest occurred in 1980, the ultramodern visitor center opened to the public in 1982, and the company is rapidly growing toward its 100,000-case-per-year production goal. Sonoma County grapes are used in four different wines made in the traditional méthode champenoise. There is also a gift shop and art gallery.

SONOMA-CUTRER VINEYARDS
4401 Slusser Rd, Windsor, CA 95492. (707) 528-1181. Tours weekdays at 2:15 by appointment; tour with tasting Saturday at 11 am by appointment. (See CSAA *Sonoma and Napa Counties* map, E-8.)

Sonoma-Cutrer is dedicated exclusively to producing estate-bottled Chardonnay. The ultra-modern facility was designed specifically for this purpose by founder Brice Cutrer Jones and winemaker Bill Bonetti. Fruit from several Sonoma County vineyards owned by the winery is hand-harvested and sorted, barrel fermented, and aged on the lees in French oak.

RODNEY STRONG VINEYARDS
12 mi N of Santa Rosa at 11455 Old Redwood Hwy (PO Box 368), Windsor, CA 95492. (800) 678-4763 or (707) 431-1533. Open daily 10 am to 5 pm for tasting. Tours daily at 11 am, 1 and 3 pm. (See CSAA *Sonoma and Napa Counties* map, D-7.)

Rodney Strong was one of the first to name vineyards on wine labels, and six of his estate-grown varietals carry vineyard designations. The building designed by architect Craig Roland (a student of Frank Lloyd Wright's) houses a skylit tasting bar, a gift shop, the winery and cellar. A walkway encircling the tasting room allows visitors to view the storage and aging area below; the lower level of the winery is designed so that winemaking operations take place in the center of the building, beneath the tasting room, and storage and aging takes place in the wings. Vertical tastings are offered weekends; more frequently in summer. A picnic area is available.

HEALDSBURG

ALDERBROOK WINERY 2306
Magnolia Dr, Healdsburg, CA 95448. (707) 433-9154. Open daily 10 am to 5 pm for tasting. Tours by appointment only. (See CSAA *Sonoma and Napa Counties* map, D-7.)

Mark Rafanelli, John Grace and Phil Staley founded Alderbrook in 1981 on this 63-acre ranch in the southernmost sector of Dry Creek Valley and rebuilt the 70-year-old redwood barn as a winery. The partners produce about 22,000 cases per year of Chardonnay, Gewürztraminer, Petite Sirah, Sauvignon Blanc and Semillon, plus a 50/50 Semillon-Sauvignon Blanc blend. The tasting room, made of pickled pine, has a picnic deck and overlooks the vineyards.

ALEXANDER VALLEY VINE-YARDS
8 mi SE of Geyserville at 8644 Hwy 128, Healdsburg, CA 95448. (707) 433-7209. Open daily 10 am to 5 pm for tasting. Tours by appointment only. (See CSAA *Sonoma and Napa Counties* map, C-8.)

Alexander Valley Vineyards lies alongside the Russian River. The small winery was built in 1975, and mature vineyards allowed production to begin immediately. The winery specializes in eight estate-bottled varietal wines. Visitors can also enjoy the setting of Cyrus Alexander's original homestead, a Sonoma County historical landmark.

BELLEROSE VINEYARD 1.4 mi W
of Healdsburg at 435 West Dry Creek

Rd, Healdsburg, CA 95448. (707) 433-1637. Open for tasting daily 11 am to 4:30 pm. Tours by appointment only. (See CSAA *Sonoma and Napa Counties* map, D-7.)

Bellerose was founded in 1979, but grape growing and winemaking on the property date from 1887. Owner and winemaker Charles Richard specializes in three wines—Cabernet Sauvignon, Merlot and Sauvignon Blanc—all blended in the Bordeaux style. Richard avoids the use of herbicides and pesticides and uses a team of Belgian draft horses in the vineyards when possible. Picnic facilities overlook Dry Creek Valley.

DAVIS BYNUM WINERY 8 mi W of Healdsburg at 8075 Westside Rd, Healdsburg, CA 95448. (707) 433-5852. Open daily 10 am to 5 pm for tasting. Tours by appointment only. (See CSAA *Sonoma and Napa Counties* map, E-7.)

Davis Bynum started his career as a vintner in 1965, when he founded his winery in the East Bay town of Albany. In 1973 the operation moved here to the River Bend Ranch in the Russian River Valley. An old hop kiln was converted to wine production, which totals 25,000 cases per year of Chardonnay, Cabernet Sauvignon, Sauvignon Blanc, Gewürztraminer, Merlot, Pinot Noir and Zinfandel. Visitors are welcome to use the picnic facilities.

CHRISTOPHER CREEK 2 mi SE of Healdsburg off Old Redwood Hwy at 641 Limerick Ln, Healdsburg, CA 95448. (707) 433-2001. Open 11 am to 5 pm Fri through Mon for tasting and tours. (See CSAA *Sonoma and Napa Counties* map, D-8.)

This winery lies on the site of the former Rancho Sotoyome, from which its

earlier, Indian name was borrowed. Founded in 1972 and bought by the Mitchell family in 1988, it is one of the smallest full-service wineries in the state. The winery produces about 2500 cases of estate-bottled Syrah and Petite Sirah per year from 10 acres of hillside vineyards. The tasting room is simple and elegant. Visitors are advised to call ahead during the winter.

Thanks to vintners growers, and county organizations, many wineries are clearly marked and easy to find. Others preserve their seclusion by blending into the countryside unannounced.

CHALK HILL WINERY 10300 Chalk Hill Rd, Healdsburg, CA 95448. (707) 838-4306. Open by appointment only for tasting and tours. (See CSAA *Sonoma and Napa Counties* map, D-8.)

Chalk Hill Winery is situated on 1100 acres owned by Frederick P. Furth, and the vineyards comprise 278 acres of the estate. The area derives its name from the chalky soil made up of ash spewed out from volcanic Mt. St. Helena at the northern end of the Napa Valley. The grapes for the winery's Chardonnay, Sauvignon Blanc and Cabernet Sauvignon are grown at an elevation of 200 to 600 feet. Guided tours and tasting are available to visitors with appointments who will be given directions to the winery by the security guard at the gated entrance.

DOMAINE ST. GEORGE WINERY & VINEYARDS 2 mi SE of Healdsburg off Old Redwood Hwy at 1141 Grant Av (PO Box 548), Healdsburg, CA 95448. (707) 433-5508. Open Mon through Fri 10 am to 4 pm for retail sales (no tasting). Tours by appointment only. (See CSAA *Sonoma and Napa Counties* map, D-7.)

The former jug-wine oriented Cambiaso winery has modernized and expanded, resulting in a shift in emphasis toward vintage-dated varietals from grapes grown in Northern California vineyards. Visitors to the hillside winery today will see a functional, modern facility located directly adjacent to the old, rustic cellar.

FERRARI-CARANO VINEYARDS AND WINERY 10 mi N of Healdsburg at 8761 Dry Creek Rd (PO Box 1549), Healdsburg, CA 95448. (707) 433-6700. Open daily 10 am to 5 pm for tasting. Tours by appointment Mon through Sat at 10 am and 2 pm.

(See CSAA *Sonoma and Napa Counties* map, B-6.)

This lavish, ultra-modern winery opened in 1987 at the foot of Lake Sonoma in northern Dry Creek Valley. Twelve separate vineyards totaling 500 acres yield the grapes for four varietals: Chardonnay, Sauvignon Blanc, Cabernet Sauvignon and Merlot. Lots of separately vinified wines are maintained for blending wines of complexity. Five acres of flower gardens provide year-round color around the Italian Villa that houses the winery and tasting room.

FIELD STONE WINERY 9 mi E of Healdsburg at 10075 Hwy 128, Healdsburg, CA 95448. (707) 433-7266. Open daily 10 am to 5 pm for tasting. Tours by appointment only. (See CSAA *Sonoma and Napa Counties* map, C-8.)

Fronted by a handsome stone wall, this small winery is tucked underground in an Alexander Valley hillside. Capacity is 12,000 cases; current offerings include five varietal wines, all estate bottled. A prearranged tour yields a comprehensive summary of winery operations. There is a gift shop, refrigerated deli items and a picnic area.

FOPPIANO VINEYARDS 2 mi S of Healdsburg at 12707 Old Redwood Hwy (PO Box 606), Healdsburg, CA 95448. (707) 433-7272. Open daily 10 am to 4:30 pm for tasting and self-guided vineyard tours. Guided winery tours by appointment only. (See CSAA *Sonoma and Napa Counties* map, D-7.)

Giovanni "John" Foppiano purchased his land in the Russian River Valley in 1896, and the oldest part of the winery, built in 1880, can be seen on tours.

Although fermentation and aging are done primarily in stainless steel tanks and small oak cooperage, a few rare redwood storage tanks that date from before Prohibition are still used with the red wines. The winery is known for its Petite Sirah but makes five additional varietal and two blended wines. Appointments are needed for winery tours, which allow visitors to taste past and current releases, plus wine from the barrel.

JOHNSON'S ALEXANDER VALLEY WINES 7 mi SE of Geyserville at 8333 Hwy 128, Healdsburg, CA 95448. (707) 433-2319. Open daily 10 am to 5 pm for tasting and tours. (See CSAA *Sonoma and Napa Counties* map, C-8.)

The Johnsons started farming in the Alexander Valley in 1952, but their first premium grapes weren't planted until 1966. A decade later the winery was completed. The rustic building is open daily for tours and tasting, and visitors are invited to picnic.

LYTTON SPRINGS WINERY 3 mi N of Healdsburg off US 101 at 650 Lytton Springs Rd, Healdsburg, CA 95448. (707) 433-7721. Open daily 10 am to 4 pm for tasting and self-guided tours. (See CSAA *Sonoma and Napa Counties* map, C-7.)

Lytton Springs Winery was founded by Dick Sherwin, who built the winery in 1977 on the Valley Vista Vineyard, where turn-of-the-century Zinfandel vines were well-known for providing grapes of high quality. The winery is now owned by Ridge Vineyards of Cupertino, which used the vineyard's fruit for their Zinfandel during the 1970s. In 1987, Cabernet Sauvignon was made in addition to the traditionally vinified Zinfandels. There is a gift shop and picnic facilities.

MAZZOCCO VINEYARDS 5 mi N of Healdsburg off US 101 at 1400 Lytton Springs Rd (PO Box 49), Healdsburg, CA 95448. (707) 431-8159. Open daily 10 am to 4 pm for tasting. Tours by appointment only. (See CSAA *Sonoma and Napa Counties* map, C-7.)

Thomas Mazzocco founded his winery in 1985 in the rolling hills between the Alexander and Dry Creek valleys. Winemaker Phyllis Zouzounis vinifies Cabernet Sauvignon, Chardonnay, Merlot, and a blended wine, plus an unfined and unfiltered Zinfandel available only at the winery. The rosebush-lined driveway leads to the tasting room, a former residential building, which overlooks a small pond.

PRESTON VINEYARDS 8 mi NW of Healdsburg at 9282 West Dry Creek Rd, Healdsburg, CA 95448. (707) 433-3372. Open weekdays noon to 4 pm, weekends 11 am to 4 pm. (See CSAA *Sonoma and Napa Counties* map, C-6.)

The Preston winery was founded in 1975 on the west side of Dry Creek Valley. Over 125 acres of family-owned vineyards contribute the fruit which is annually transformed into 30,000 cases of Sauvignon Blanc, Chenin Blanc, Cabernet Sauvignon, Zinfandel and a proprietary red wine. The winery was originally housed in an old prune dehydrating shed; in 1982, a modern new structure styled along traditional lines was completed. Picnic facilities are also available.

QUIVIRA VINEYARDS 5.5 mi NW of Healdsburg at 4900 West Dry Creek Rd, Healdsburg, CA 95448. (707) 431-8333. Open 10 am to 4:30 pm for tasting; closed major holidays. Tours by appointment only. (See CSAA *Sonoma and Napa Counties* map, C-6.)

Quivira, named after the mythical civilization that enticed 16th- and 17th-century explorers, was founded in 1981 and has since grown into a 76-acre, 20,000-case-per-year enterprise. Zinfandel and Sauvignon Blanc are the house specialties, with Cabernet Sauvignon added in the fall of 1990. The wines are made in a modern cedar and redwood building on the west side of Dry Creek Valley. Shaded picnic facilities overlook the valley.

SIMI WINERY, INC. 1 mi N of Healdsburg at 16275 Healdsburg Av (PO Box 698), Healdsburg, CA 95448. (707) 433-6981. Open daily 10 am to 4:30 pm for tasting. Tours daily at 11 am, 1 and 3 pm. (See CSAA *Sonoma and Napa Counties* map, C-7.)

The winery that the Simi brothers began in 1890 underwent a massive modernization in the 1970s. Today the winery produces seven premium varietals: Cabernet Sauvignon, Chardonnay, Sauvignon Blanc, Chenin Blanc, Rose of Cabernet Sauvignon, Semillon and Muscat Canelli. Visitors to the winery can take a 45-minute guided tour of the crushers, fermenting room and aging cellars. Picnicking is welcome.

WILLIAM WHEELER WINERY 130 Plaza St, Healdsburg, CA 95448. (707) 433-8786. Open daily 11 am to 4 pm for tasting and self-guided tours. (See CSAA *Sonoma and Napa Counties* map, D-7.)

The Wheelers are Dry Creek Valley growers who opened a winery in 1981. They produce about 14,000 cases per year of Chardonnay, Cabernet Sauvignon, Merlot, Sauvignon Blanc, Zinfandel and white Zinfandel from their own and purchased grapes. Visitors to the downtown Healdsburg tasting room can tour the fermentation area

and wine cellar. An annual open house is held over the Thanksgiving weekend.

WHITE OAK VINEYARDS in Healdsburg at 208 Hayden St, Healdsburg, CA 95448. (707) 433-8429. Open for tasting Fri through Sun 10 am to 4 pm. Tours by appointment only. (See CSAA *Sonoma and Napa Counties* map, D-7.)

White Oak was founded in 1981 by Bill Myers, who built his winery after moving to Healdsburg from Anchorage, Alaska, where he worked as a salmon fisherman and building contractor. Today, the winery produces 14,000 cases annually of six varietal wines in a small, modern facility. Grapes come from estate-owned and contracted vineyards in the Alexander, Dry Creek and Russian River valleys.

Wineries Open For Tasting Only

The following wineries in Healdsburg have tasting rooms on the premises but do not offer tours.

BELVEDERE WINERY 4 mi W of Healdsburg at 4035 Westside Rd, Healdsburg, CA 95448. (707) 433-8236. Open daily 10 am to 4:30 pm. Gift shop, art gallery, picnic facilities. (See CSAA *Sonoma and Napa Counties* map, D-7.)

CLOS DU BOIS 5 Fitch St, Healdsburg, CA 95448. (707) 433-5576, (800) 222-3189. Open daily 10 am to 4:30 pm. Closed major holidays. (See CSAA *Sonoma and Napa Counties* map, D-7.)

DRY CREEK VINEYARD 4 mi NW of Healdsburg at Dry Creek and Lambert Bridge rds (PO Box T), Healdsburg, CA 95448. (707) 433-1000. Open daily 10:30 am to 4:30 pm. (See CSAA *Sonoma and Napa Counties* map, C-7.)

Michelle De Lude

Hopland was named for the hops grown so successfully in Mendocino and northern Sonoma counties. Built in 1905, these restored buildings have provided a name and a home for the Hop Kiln Winery since 1975.

THE HOP KILN WINERY 6 mi SW of Healdsburg at 6050 Westside Rd, Healdsburg, CA 95448. (707) 433-6491. Open daily 10 am to 5 pm. Art gallery, picnic area beside large pond. (See CSAA *Sonoma and Napa Counties* map, E-7.)

MILL CREEK VINEYARDS 1401 Westside Rd (PO Box 758), Healdsburg, CA 95448. (707) 431-2121. Open daily 10 am to 4:30 pm Apr through Dec, noon to 4:30 pm Fri through Mon Jan through Mar. (See CSAA *Sonoma and Napa Counties* map, D-7.)

ROCHIOLI VINEYARDS & WINERY 6 mi SW of Healdsburg at 6192 Westside Rd, Healdsburg, CA 95448. (707) 433-2305. Open daily 10 am to 5 pm for tasting. Tours by appointment only. (See CSAA *Sonoma and Napa Counties* map, E-7.)

SAUSAL WINERY 7 mi NE of Healdsburg at 7370 Hwy 128,

Healdsburg, CA 95448. (707) 433-2285. Open daily 10 am to 4 pm. (See CSAA *Sonoma and Napa Counties* map, C-8.)

ROBERT STEMMLER VINEYARDS 4 mi NW of Healdsburg off Dry Creek Rd at 3805 Lambert Bridge Rd, Healdsburg, CA 95448. (707) 433-6334. Open daily 10:30 am to 4:30 pm. (See CSAA *Sonoma and Napa Counties* map, C-7.)

GEYSERVILLE

GEYSER PEAK WINERY 1 mi N of Geyserville off US 101 at 22281 Chianti Rd, Geyserville, CA 95441. (707) 857-9400, (800) 255-9463. Open daily 10 am to 5 pm for tasting; closed major holidays. Tours by appointment only. (See CSAA *Sonoma and Napa Counties* map, B-7.)

Geyser Peak Winery was founded in 1880 by winemaker Augustus Quitzow, who constructed the winery on its hillside opposing Geyser Peak mountain two years later. The impressive ivy-covered buildings have stained glass windows, and there is a picnic area beside the winery and a fountain at the entrance. Now owned by the Trione family, the winery produces a large number of varietal wines and a red Meritage blend under winemaker Daryl Groom. Groom was the first winemaker to produce the traditional Australian blend of Semillon and Chardonnay in the United States. Refrigerated deli items are sold in the tasting room and gift shop.

Wineries Open for Tasting Only
The following wineries in the Geyserville area have tasting rooms on the premises but do not offer tours.

CHATEAU SOUVERAIN 5 mi N of Healdsburg off US 101 and Independence Ln at 400 Souverain Rd (PO Box 528), Geyserville, CA 95441. (707) 433-3141. Open Thu through

Mon 9:30 am to 5 pm. Restaurant, cafe, gift shop. (See CSAA *Sonoma and Napa Counties* map, C-7.)

MURPHY-GOODE ESTATE WINERY 5 mi SE of Geyserville at 4001 Hwy 128 (PO Box 158), Geyserville, CA 95441. (707) 431-7644. Open for tasting 10:30 a.m. to 4:30 p.m. Closed major holidays. Gift shop.

NERVO WINERY 19550 Geyserville Av (PO Box 25), Geyserville, CA 95441. (707) 857-3417. Open daily 10 am to 5 pm except major holidays. Picnic facilities available. (See CSAA *Sonoma and Napa Counties* map, C-7.)

J. PEDRONCELLI WINERY 1 mi N of Geyserville at 1220 Canyon Rd, Geyserville, CA 95441. (707) 857-3531. Open daily 10 am to 5 pm for tasting. Tours by appointment. (See CSAA *Sonoma and Napa Counties* map, C-6.)

For Chateau Souverain, architect John Davis, who also designed Rutherford Hill Winery, blended the shape of Sonoma County's familiar hop kilns with that of a French Chateau.

TRENTADUE WINERY, 3 mi S of Geyserville at 19170 Geyserville Av, Geyserville, CA 95441. (707) 433-3104. Open daily 10 am to 5 pm. Gift shop, refrigerated deli items, picnic area. (See CSAA *Sonoma and Napa Counties* map, C-7.)

CLOVERDALE

J. FRITZ WINERY 3 mi S of Cloverdale at 24691 Dutcher Creek Rd, Cloverdale, CA 95425. (707) 894-3389. Open daily 10:30 am to 4:30 pm for tasting. Tours by appointment. (See CSAA *Sonoma and Napa Counties* map, B-6.)

Jay and Barbara Fritz built their winery in 1979 and specialize in Zinfandel, Dry Creek Valley Cabernet Sauvignon, Chardonnay and Sauvignon Blanc. Informal tours are conducted by the winemaking and cellar staff whenever possible, and visitors are welcome to picnic on the grounds overlooking the vineyards.

Winery Open for Tasting Only

The following winery in Cloverdale has a tasting room on the premises but does not offer tours.

PASTORI WINERY 23189 Geyserville Av, Cloverdale, CA 95425. (707) 857-3418. Open daily 9 am to 5 pm. (See CSAA *Sonoma and Napa Counties* map, B-6.)

MENDOCINO COUNTY

HOPLAND

FETZER VINEYARDS at the Valley Oaks Food and Wine Center, 1 mi E of Hopland at jct of US 101 and SR 175; 13601 East Side Rd (PO Box 611), Hopland CA 95449. (707) 744-1250 (winery and garden hospitality),

744-1737 (tasting room). Open 9 am to 5 pm daily for tasting. Weekend garden and winery tours by appointment at 11 am, 1 and 3 pm. (See CSAA *North Bay Counties* map.)

Bernard Fetzer established his Redwood Valley Winery in 1958, using his experience as a lumberman to build it next to his family's residence. Now owned by Brown-Forman, the winery produces vintage-dated varietals, including a growing volume of organic wines, from its own and other Mendocino and Lake County vineyards. Visitors to the Hopland site can arrange to see Fetzer's four-and-a-half-acre organic garden, which contains about 1300 varieties of fruits and vegetables, on weekend tours.

MCDOWELL VALLEY VINE-YARDS PO Box 449, Hopland, CA 95449. (707) 744-1053. Winery open weekdays by appointment only for tasting and tours. Tasting room open daily; located on US-101 in Hopland. Hours 10 am to 5 pm daily from May 2 through December 31, noon to 5 pm weekdays and 11 am to 5 pm weekends rest of year. Closed major holidays. (See CSAA *North Bay Counties* map.)

The McDowell Valley is a small alluvial benchland in southeastern Mendocino County. It is host to only one winery: McDowell Valley Vineyards. Richard and Karen Keehn have been growers here since 1970; in 1979, they constructed a winery that uses solar power. They produce Grenache and Syrah, their Rhone varietals, along with Cabernet Sauvignon, Chardonnay, Sauvignon Blanc, and Zinfandel from the estate's 400 acres of contiguous vineyards. Visitors with appointments are given tours of the facility. The Hopland tasting room has a gift shop and picnic facilities.

MILANO WINERY 14594 S Hwy 101, Hopland, CA 95449. (707) 744-

1396. Open daily 10 am to 5 pm for tasting. Tours by appointment only. (See CSAA *North Bay Counties* map.)

In the early 1900s, grower Vincenzo Milone settled in Hopland, where the southern Mendocino County countryside reminded him of his home in Brindisi, Italy. In 1976, his grandson, Jim Milone, began converting the family's hop kiln into the family winery. Today, Jim and his father Frank work side by side to produce small lots of varietal wines from the family vineyards. The emphasis is on Chardonnay, Cabernet Sauvignon, Zinfandel and late-harvest dessert wines. Visitors are welcome in the tasting and sales room and picnic area; tours must be arranged in advance.

PHILO

GREENWOOD RIDGE VINE-YARDS Tasting room located 3 mi N of Philo at 5501 Hwy 128 open daily 10 am to 6 pm in summer, 10 am to 5 pm rest of year. Closed Thanksgiving, Christmas and New Year's Day. (707) 895-2002. Tours of winery by appointment. (See CSAA *North Bay Counties* map.)

This tiny winery opened in 1980 on a 1400-foot-high ridge adjacent to the Anderson Valley. The eight-acre vineyard planted in 1972 to Riesling, Merlot and Cabernet Sauvignon grapes has grown to twelve, and the crop supplies the winery with some of the fruit for its 6000-case annual output. Each July, the winery hosts the light-hearted California Wine Tasting Championships (see *Annual Events*).

HANDLEY CELLARS 6 mi NW of Philo at 3151 SR 128; PO Box 66, Philo, CA 95466. (707) 895-3876, 895-2190. Open for tasting daily 11 am to 6 pm during daylight savings, to 5

pm rest of year. Tours by appointment. (See CSAA *North Bay Counties* map.)

Handley began in 1982 as a small family winery in the basement of the owner's home. It has grown: Now more than 15,000 cases a year of Chardonnay, Gewürztraminer, Pinot Noir, Sauvignon Blanc and méthode champenoise sparkling wine are produced from grapes grown in the Anderson and Dry Creek valleys. A modern wooden winery and tasting room were completed in 1987. Picnicking is available, and the owner's collection of folk art may be viewed in the tasting room.

HUSCH VINEYARDS 5 mi NW of Philo at 4400 SR 128, Philo, CA 95466. (707) 895-3216. Open daily 10 am to 6 pm in summer, to 5 pm rest of year, for tasting and self-guided vineyard tours. Winery tours by appointment only. (See CSAA *North Bay Counties* map.)

The winery began in 1971 on a 23-acre plot in the cool Anderson Valley. Anthony Husch and his family crushed their grapes on the patio of their home until the 1974 winery building was built. Now owned by the Oswald family, the small winery produces its varietal wines from estate-grown Gewürztraminer, Chardonnay, Sauvignon Blanc, Chenin Blanc, Cabernet Sauvignon and Pinot Noir grapes. A brochure available in the tasting room directs the visitor on a tour of the vineyard. Picnic tables are set under grape arbors.

LAZY CREEK VINEYARDS N of Philo off SR 128 (PO Box 176), Philo, CA 95466. (707) 895-3623. Open by appointment only for tasting and tours. (See CSAA *North Bay Counties* Area map.)

During his restaurant career, Hans Kobler grew increasingly disappointed that no one was making the kind of wines he enjoyed most, so when he and his wife Teresia began planning their move from the busy city, he chose a location where he could realize his dream of crafting Alsatian-style Gewürztraminer in addition to Pinot Noir and Chardonnay. Lazy Creek was the third bonded winery in the Anderson Valley, and production is only 4000 cases per year. Those who wish an in-depth view of the winery's facilities and the winemaker's philosophy should call for an appointment and directions to the one-lane dirt road leading to the winery.

NAVARRO VINEYARDS 3 mi N of Philo at 5601 Hwy 128 (PO Box 47), Philo, CA 95466. (707) 895-3686. Open daily for tasting 10 am to 6 pm in summer, to 5 pm in winter. Tours by appointment only. (See CSAA *North Bay Counties* map.)

The winery facilities at Navarro Vineyards are located in a refurbished old barn, flanked by stainless steel fermentors and backed by 60 acres of terraced vineyards. Ted Bennett produces 16,000 cases per year of premium Riesling, Cabernet Sauvignon, Chardonnay, Pinot Noir and the house specialty, Gewürztraminer. These are offered in the wooden tasting room, which opened in 1980; picnic facilities are also available.

OBESTER WINERY .75 mi S of Philo at 9200 SR 128, Philo, CA 95466. (707) 895-3814. Open daily 10 am to 5 pm for tasting. Tours by appointment only. (See CSAA *North Bay Counties Area* map.)

Unable to expand their Half Moon Bay facility because of zoning restrictions, Paul and Sandy Obester purchased 85 acres in the Anderson Valley, where seven acres are currently planted to equal parts Chardonnay, Gewürzt-

raminer, and Pinot Noir. The winery also produces apple juice from orchards on the property and non-alcoholic Gewürztraminer grape juice in addition to other gourmet foods. A gazebo, picnic tables, and organic herb and vegetable garden frames the warm yellow farmhouse that houses the winery and the maple- and fir-paneled tasting room. Tasting is offered daily, and tours are given by appointment.

ROEDERER ESTATE 5 mi N of Philo at 4501 SR 128 (PO Box 67), Philo, CA 95466. (707) 895-2288. Open Thu through Mon 11 am to 4 pm for tasting. Tours by appointment only. (See CSAA *North Bay Counties Area* map.)

Champagne Louis Roederer of France searched two years before purchasing 580 acres of land in the Anderson Valley for its California expansion. The vineyards were planted in 1982, and the first sparkling wine was released six years later. Visitors may sample the wines during regular hours, and advance arrangements should be made for those who wish to tour the facility.

SCHARFFENBERGER CELLARS 8501 Hwy 128, Philo, CA 95466. (707) 895-2065. Tasting room open daily 11 am to 5 pm for tasting. Winery open by appointment only. (See CSAA *North Bay Counties* map.)

This méthode champenoise sparkling wine facility vinifies Chardonnay and Pinot Noir that comes from vineyards in the Anderson Valley, California's coolest viticultural region. It was established in 1981 by John Scharffenberger and is associated with Champagne Pommery and Champagne Lanson of France. The winery's tasting room and winery is located on 685 acres in downtown Philo and is open daily for tasting. Picnic facilities are available.

UKIAH

DUNNEWOOD VINEYARDS & WINERY 2399 N State St, Ukiah, CA 95470. (707) 462-2987. Open daily 10 am to 5 pm for tasting. Tours by appointment at 10:30 daily. (See CSAA *North Bay Counties* map.)

Dunnewood Vineyards occupies the facilities of the former Cresta Blanca Winery founded in the 1880s by Charles Wetmore; the Cresta Blanca brand and the winery was purchased by Guild Wineries and Distilleries (makers of Cook's sparkling wine) in the late 1960s, and Guild in turn was bought by Canandaigua Wine Company. Fruit for 120,000 cases of wine annually comes from vineyards in Mendocino, Napa and Sonoma counties, and production is expected to increase to 250,000 cases by 1995. Chardonnay composes about half of the winery's releases, with Merlot and Cabernet Sauvignon following, and small amounts of Gamay Beaujolais, Pinot Noir, Sauvignon Blanc and white Zinfandel. Tours of the facility last about an hour.

HIDDEN CELLARS 2 mi W off US 101 at 1500 Ruddick-Cunningham Rd, Ukiah; PO Box 448, Talmage, CA 95481. (707) 462-0301. Open daily Jun through Sep, 11 am to 4 pm; weekdays 11 am to 4 pm rest of year. (See CSAA *North Bay Counties* map.)

Dennis Patton was a local farmer and home winemaker when he founded Hidden Cellars in 1981. He started the first winery on Mill Creek with a hand-operated basket press and a few used dairy tanks. In 1983, he moved the operations to Hildreth Ranch, where he and winemaker Greg Graziano produce Chardonnay, Zinfandel, Sauvignon Blanc, Johannisberg Riesling, and sometimes a late harvest Riesling. All wines are made from Mendocino County

grapes, and production is now 12,000 cases per year. Visitors are welcome to picnic in the tree-shaded picnic area.

PARDUCCI WINE CELLARS 3 mi N of Ukiah at 501 Parducci Rd, Ukiah, CA 95482. (707) 462-3828. Open daily 9 am to 5 pm in winter, 9 am to 6 pm in summer. (See CSAA *North Bay Counties* map.)

The winery founded by the late Adolph Parducci in 1931 is now managed by his family, which has placed increasing emphasis on the production of premium varietal wines. The winemaking philosophy allows grapes to become wine with as little human intervention as possible. A gravity-flow system eliminates the need for pumping, "settling out" is preferred to filtering, and handling is kept to a minimum. The wines can be sampled in the tasting room, located in front of the cellars. There is a gift shop, art gallery, and picnic facilities, and informative 30-minute guided tours are conducted hourly beginning at 10 a.m. with the last tour at 4 p.m.

TIJSSELING VINEYARDS and TYLAND VINEYARDS 2150 McNab Ranch Rd, Ukiah, CA 95482. (707) 462-1810 weekdays, 462-1034 weekends. Open summer weekends 11 am to 5 pm for tasting. Tours by appointment. (See CSAA *North Bay Counties* map.)

Architectural engineer and contractor Dick Tijsseling began growing grapes in Mendocino County in 1970. In 1975 he acquired a 70-acre ranch and four years later built his winery at Tyland Vineyards where he produces wine for the Canadian market. His parents had owned the 8000-acre McNab ranch adjacent to Tyland since 1965, and in 1981 he persuaded them to build a winery. About one-third of Tijsseling's production is méthode champenoise sparkling wine, another third is premium varietal wine (Cabernet Sauvignon, Chardonnay, Sauvignon Blanc and a limited amount of Petite Sirah), and another third is blended table wine. Visitors are welcome in the tasting room on summer weekends and should call ahead if they wish a tour. A picnic area is located next to the tasting room.

REDWOOD VALLEY

FREY VINEYARDS 14000 Tomki Rd, Redwood Valley, CA 95470. (707) 485-5177. Open daily by appointment only for tasting and tours. (See CSAA *North Bay Counties* map.)

The Frey family operates California's first and largest organic winery on their ranch near the head of the Russian River in Redwood Valley. The vineyards are dry farmed without insecticides or herbicides, and the three white and three red wines are made without chemical additives.

KONRAD ESTATE WINERY 8 mi N of Ukiah off US 101 at 3620 Road B, Redwood Valley, CA 95470. (707) 485-0323. Open daily 10 am to 5 pm for tasting and tours. (See CSAA *North Bay Counties* map.)

Konrad Estate Winery is located near the north end of California's northernmost coastal growing region, on an 1100-foot plateau with extensive views over Redwood Valley and Lake Mendocino. The winery was founded in 1982 and today produces 8000 cases per year of varietal and proprietary bottlings.

Winery Open For Tasting Only
The following winery in the Redwood Valley area has a tasting room on the premises but does not offer tours.

WEIBEL WINERY 5 mi N of Ukiah at 7051 N State St (PO Box 367),

Redwood Valley, CA 95470. (707) 485-0321. Open daily 9 am to 5 pm. Picnic area. (See CSAA *North Bay Counties* map.)

LAKE COUNTY
Kelseyville, Lakeport and Lower Lake

KENDALL-JACKSON WINERY 600 Mathews Rd, Lakeport, CA 95453. (707) 263-5299. Open Tue through Sun 11 am to 5 pm for tasting and tours (call for winter hours). (See CSAA *North Bay Counties* map.)

Grapes from many of California's viticultural regions are used to make over 400,000 cases annually of varietal wines at this rapidly growing, functionally modern Lake County facility. Five white and five red varietals are produced; an 85-acre vineyard adjoins the wooden tasting room. A large, shaded lawn may be used for picnicking.

KONOCTI WINERY at jct of SR 29 and Thomas Dr (PO Box 890), Kelseyville, CA 95451. (707) 279-4395. Open Mon through Sat 10 am to 5 pm, Sun 11 am to 5 pm for tasting. Tours by appointment only. (See CSAA *North Bay Counties* map.)

Konocti is a cooperative winery founded by an association of Lake County growers and named after Mt. Konocti, the area's 4200-foot inactive volcano. Grapes from 400 acres of vineyards are made into varietal wines in a functional, insulated metal building which sits in the midst of an experimental vineyard. The first crush occurred in 1974; now the capacity stands at 50,000 cases per year. The gift shop and tasting room are open daily, and visitors are invited to tour the facilities and picnic nearby.

Napa and Sonoma Valleys

The Napa and Sonoma valleys are the best known of California's wine districts. Divided by the Mayacamas mountain range, they have similar weather conditions, with sunny days tempered by cooling marine breezes and fog. These conditions are best for premium grape varieties such as Cabernet Sauvignon, Pinot Noir and Chardonnay.

Winemaking began in Sonoma when the Franciscan fathers founded their mission there. Their success eventually attracted Agoston Haraszthy, who planted his European vines at Buena Vista. Another Sonoma landmark dates back to the turn of the century, when Samuele Sebastiani launched the town's biggest winery. Jack London State Park is located in the valley, which the writer made famous in his 1913 novel, The Valley of the Moon. Sonoma Valley and Sonoma Mountain are both viticultural appellations of this area, as is the Carneros district, which lies partly in Sonoma County and partly in Napa.

East of Sonoma lies the Napa Valley, California's most renowned wine region. The acclaimed "Rutherford Bench" area lies along the western side of SR 29 from Dwyer Road in the south to Grgich Hills in the north. Along the Silverado Trail the Stags Leap district extends south from Yountville Cross Road to just beyond Clos du Val. Many Napa Valley wineries, including Charles Krug, Beaulieu, and Beringer have been producing premium wines for nearly a hundred years or more, and the wine boom of the 1980s added a host of newer names. Tourism has also increased dramatically, and the summer and weekend visitor will often encounter very crowded roads and tasting rooms in the Napa Valley.

To locate the wineries in this section, refer to the CSAA Sonoma and Napa Counties map; more detailed maps of this area can be obtained in person at any office of the California State Automobile Association.

ANNUAL EVENTS

Exact dates, prices and information about the events listed below may be verified by calling the telephone numbers shown. Some wineries also individually sponsor special brunches, dinners, and summer concerts. Those interested in the events sponsored by a particular winery should call that winery and ask if a calendar of events is available.

MARCH—
Heart of the Valley Barrel Tasting
various locations in Sonoma Valley. (707) 833-5891. St. Francis, Arrowood, Glen Ellen, Kenwood, Landmark and Chateau

St. Jean are among the participating wineries. $10 includes a souvenir glass that admits you to activities, displays, and tastings of unreleased wines from the barrel, component wines and hors d'oeuvres. Tickets must be ordered in advance by calling any participating winery or Karen Leonard at the number above.

MAY—
Spring Mountain Open House, *St. Helena.* (707) 963-1616. The wineries of Spring Mountain are generally closed to the public, but during one weekend

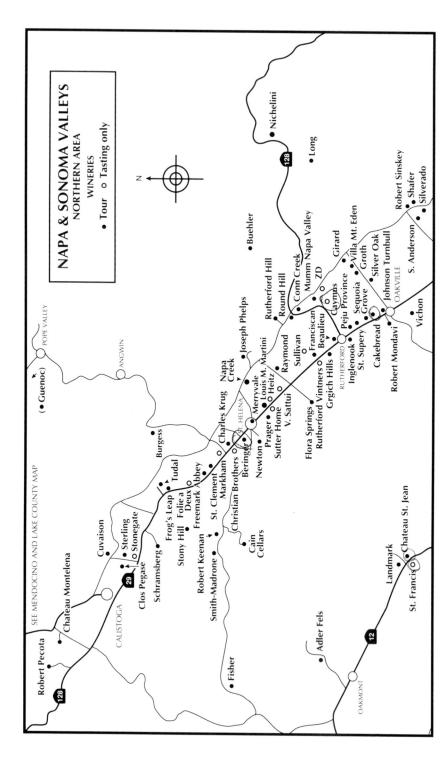

NAPA & SONOMA VALLEYS
NORTHERN AREA
WINERIES
● Tour   ○ Tasting only

N

SEE MENDOCINO AND LAKE COUNTY MAP

POPE VALLEY

(● Guenoc)

ANGWIN

Nichelini

Long

128

Buehler

Robert Pecota

128

Chateau Montelena

CALISTOGA

29

Clos Pegase

Schramsberg

Cuvaison

Sterling
○ Stongate

Frog's Leap
Tudal

Stony Hill   Folie a
Deux
Freemark Abbey

Robert Keenan

Smith-Madrone

St. Clement
Markham

Christian Brothers
Beringer
Newton
Prager

Sutter Home

Cain
Cellars

Burgess

Charles Krug
ST. HELENA

Napa
Creek

Merryvale
Louis M. Martini
○ Heitz
V. Sattui

Joseph Phelps

Rutherford Hill
Round Hill

Conn Creek
Mumm Napa Valley
ZD

Girard

Villa Mt. Eden
Groth
Silver Oak
Johnson Turnbull

Robert Sinskey
Shafer
Silverado

S. Anderson

OAKVILLE

Vichon

Raymond
Sullivan

Franciscan
Beaulieu

Caymus
Peju Province

Sequoia
Grove

St. Supery
Cakebread

Robert Mondavi

RUTHERFORD

Inglenook

Flora Springs
Rutherford Vintners
Grgich Hills

Fisher

Adler Fels

Landmark

Chateau St. Jean
St. Francis

12

OAKMONT

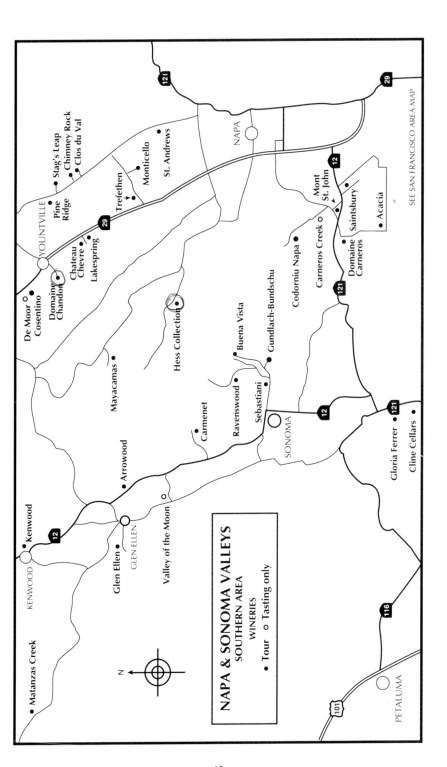

NAPA & SONOMA VALLEYS
SOUTHERN AREA
WINERIES
• Tour   ○ Tasting only

SEE SAN FRANCISCO AREA MAP

65

Easily seen from the highway, Domaine Carneros takes its name from the Carneros region. Lying at the southern end of the Napa and Sonoma valleys, this region is best known for its Chardonnay and Pinot Noir grapes.

in May they open for wine tasting and conversations with winemakers on style, technique, terrain and grape varieties.

JUNE—

Ox Roast *Sonoma.* (707) 938-4626. This family-oriented festival centers around a tri-tip, oxburger and ox-dog barbecue at Sonoma Plaza. Wine tasting, art displays, live bands and games for children round out the day.

JULY—

Old-Fashioned 4th of July *Sonoma.* (707) 938-4626. A parade provides excitement and color joined at Sonoma Plaza by games, food and wine tasting and live music.

Salute to the Arts *Sonoma.* (707) 938-1133. Sonoma Plaza is the site of this celebration of fine arts, culinary arts and music. Sonoma area restaurants, pro-

duce, wine, and seafood provide tasting samples, and three stages provide the locations for concerts and plays. Call above number for prices and other information.

AUGUST—

Wine and Art Fair *various locations in Sonoma Valley.* (707) 833-4666. Advance purchase of tickets to this family-oriented event are suggested. A $5 souvenir glass serves as your passport to the arts and crafts areas set up at each winery. A horse-drawn wagon carries visitors between two wineries, local volunteer organizations provide food, and children will have special activities and attractions. Call Penny at the number above.

SEPTEMBER—

Valley of the Moon Vintage Festival *Sonoma.* (707) 966-2109. Events range from the blessing of the grapes to a children's parade and grape stomping.

DECEMBER—

Victorian Christmas Caroling Party
Rutherford at St. Supery. (707) 963-4507. Costumed carolers entertain on the veranda of the Atkinson House and in various parts of the winery; refreshments include mulled wine, hot chocolate, cookies, punch and popcorn. Call for reservations and ticket prices.

NAPA VALLEY

NAPA AREA

ACACIA WINERY 4 mi SW of Napa at 2750 Las Amigas Rd, Napa 94559. (707) 226-9991. Open by appointment for tasting and tours. (See CSAA *Sonoma and Napa Counties* map, H-12.)

Acacia was founded in 1979 to produce Chardonnay and Pinot Noir from grapes grown in the Carneros region of the southern Napa Valley. The cool climate and careful viticultural practices combine to produce optimum fruit, and Acacia won immediate renown for its relatively small quantities of vineyard-designated varietals. The modern winery is located on a hill surrounded by the Marina Vineyard, which produces the winery's estate Chardonnay.

CHIMNEY ROCK WINERY 1.5 mi N of Oak Knoll Av at 5350 Silverado Trail, Napa 94558. (707) 257-2641. Open daily 10 am to 5 pm for tasting; $3 tasting fee includes souvenir glass or credit toward purchase. Tours by appointment only. Closed major holidays.

Hack and Stella Wilson bought the Chimney Rock Golf Course in 1980, took out part of the back nine and put in grapevines, joining nine other wineries in the celebrated Stags Leap district. Production is about 15,000 cases per year with the emphasis on Cabernet Sauvignon, but the winery also grows and vinifies Chardonnay, Sauvignon Blanc, Merlot and Cabernet Franc. Tours are tailored to the interest and experience level of the individual, and instead of arranging tasting at the end of the tour, different wines are poured during the tour as it progresses. The winery, built five years after the first crush, is adorned by a replica of a frieze of Ganymede, cupbearer to the gods, created for the Groot Constantia winery in Africa by sculptor Anton Anreith.

CLOS DU VAL WINE COMPANY, LTD. 5 mi N of Napa at 5330 Silverado Trail (PO Box 4350), Napa 94558. (707) 252-6711. Open daily 10 am to 5 pm for tasting; $3 fee. Tours by appointment. (See CSAA *Sonoma and Napa Counties* map, F-13.)

Launched in 1972, Clos du Val combines winemaker Bernard Portet's French enological background with American technology. The winery produces Merlot, Zinfandel, Cabernet Sauvignon, and Semillon varietal wines from estate vineyards located adjacent to the early-California-style winery. Pinot Noir and Chardonnay are produced from their vineyards in the Carneros district.

CODORNIU NAPA 3.5 mi W of SR 29 off SR 12/121 via Dealy Ln at 1345 Henry Rd, Napa 94558. (707) 224-1668. Open 10 am to 5 pm Mon through Thu, to 3 pm Fri through Sun for tasting and tours; $4 tasting fee per glass. (See CSAA *Sonoma and Napa Counties* map, G-12.)

The Codorniu family made Spain's first méthode champenoise sparkling wine in

1872, and in 1991 they opened their first sparkling wine facility outside Spain in the Carneros district of Napa County. The earth-covered building, designed by Domingo Triay, is covered with grasses indigenous to California. A striking prism window, fountains, falls and pools adorn the entrance to the winery. Inside, exhibits of changing and permanent artwork and antique wine-making equipment can be seen on self-guided tours, and guided tours cover the history, architecture and winemaking techniques of the winery in detail.

The vivid contrast of avant-garde architecture and antique wine-making equipment provides a lively experience for visitors to the Codorniu Napa Winery.

DOMAINE CARNEROS 5.5 mi SW of Napa off SR 12/121 at 1240 Duhig Rd (PO Box 5420), Napa 94581. (707) 257-0101. Open for tasting daily 10 am to 6 pm Jun to Nov; Fri through Tue 10:30 am to 4:30 pm rest of year; $4 tasting fee per glass includes hors d'oeuvres. Tours on weekends every hour on the hour, last one leaves at 3 pm; tours weekdays at 11 am, 1 and 3 pm. (See CSAA *Sonoma and Napa Counties* map, H-12.)

The impressive building overlooking the state highway in the Carneros region was inspired by the Chateau de la Marquetterie and houses a joint venture of Champagne Taittinger of France, Kobrand Corporation, and Peter Ordway (the original owner of the vineyards). This méthode champenoise sparkling wine facility was founded in 1987, and production now stands at 45,000 cases per year using grapes grown only in the Carneros region.

THE HESS COLLECTION WIN-ERY at 4411 Redwood Rd (PO Box 4140), Napa 94558. (707) 255-1144. Open daily 10 am to 4 pm for tasting and self-guided tours; $2.50 tasting fee.

Swiss entrepreneur Donald Hess chose the steep sides of Mount Veeder for his venture into California winemaking. Bronze plaques and a brochure guide visitors to views overlooking winery operations and two upper floors of art galleries (accessible by stair and elevator). A 12-minute audiovisual presentation screens every half hour and shows the seasonal challenges unique in mountain vineyards. 285 of the more than 900 acres of property are planted to Chardonnay and Cabernet Sauvignon (the winery's two varietals), and small amounts of red Bordeaux grapes are grown for blending purposes. The fine collection of contemporary artwork is not presented as an introduction for those unfamiliar with the genre, but a catalog of the exhibited work may be purchased.

MAYACAMAS VINEYARDS 10 mi W of SR 29 at 1155 Lokoya Rd, Napa 94558. (707) 224-4030. Open by appointment for tasting and tours. (See CSAA *Sonoma and Napa Counties* map, G-12.)

Mayacamas was founded high on the slopes of Mount Veeder in 1889 by John Fisher, a professional sword engraver and pickle merchant; he sold his new business after the turn of the century. There-after, the winery changed hands several times; Robert and Elinor Travers have owned the property since 1968. They have concentrated on the production of renowned Cabernet Sauvignon and Chardonnay wines, primarily from Mayacamas-grown grapes, and they also produce Sauvignon Blanc and Pinot Noir.

MONTICELLO CELLARS 5 mi N of Napa off SR 29 and Oak Knoll Av at 4242 Big Ranch Rd, Napa 94558. (707) 253-2802. Open daily 10 am to 4:30 pm for tasting; $2.50 tasting fee includes souvenir glass. Tours at 10:30 am, 12:30 and 2:30 pm. (See CSAA *Sonoma and Napa Counties* map, G-13.)

The vineyards at Monticello were planted to white grapes in 1970 and, when they matured, sold to local wineries. In 1980, the owners formed Monticello Cellars and began producing wines from their annual harvests. A modern winery was built in 1982 to handle the 18,000-case-per-year output of Chardonnay, Cabernet Sauvignon, Merlot, Pinot Noir and late-harvest Semillon. The hospitality center was built to resemble Thomas Jefferson's home in Virginia, the winery's namesake. Picnic facilities are available.

MONT ST. JOHN CELLARS 3 mi SW of Napa off SR 12 at 5400 Old

Sonoma Rd, Napa 94559. (707) 255-8864. Open daily 10 am to 5 pm for tasting. Tours by appointment only. (See CSAA *Sonoma and Napa Counties* map, H-13.)

Long-time Napa Valley grower and winemaker Louis Bartolucci and his son Andrea acquired 160 acres of vineyard land in the Carneros region in 1971. The estate vineyard, Madonna Vineyard, is well known for its Pinot Noir and Chardonnay grapes; the winery also produces Cabernet Sauvignon, Riesling and Gewürztraminer. There is a gift shop and picnic area.

ST. ANDREW'S VINEYARD 1 mi N of Trancas St at 2921 Silverado Trail (PO Box 4107), Napa 94558. (707) 252-6748. Open weekends 10 am to 5 pm and weekdays by appointment for tasting, retail sales and tours. (See CSAA *Sonoma and Napa Counties* map, G-13.)

A sister company of Clos du Val Winery in Napa and Taltarni Vineyards in Australia, the 63-acre St. Andrew's Vineyard was planted in 1972 and has been in John Goelet's capable hands since 1989. The winery itself was built in 1979, and the first wines were produced the following year. Production is limited to Chardonnay and Sauvignon Blanc.

SAINTSBURY 4 mi SW of Napa off SR 12/121 at 1500 Los Carneros Av, Napa 94559. (707) 252-0592. Open weekdays by appointment for tasting and tours. (See CSAA *Sonoma and Napa Counties* map, H-13.)

Saintsbury wines were first made in 1981, and a modern winery was completed in the Napa Valley's Carneros district in 1983. Grapes are purchased from cool local vineyards and are carefully processed and aged in French oak

cooperage. The owners/winemakers are devoting their efforts to Burgundian varietals: at present, 40,000 cases of Chardonnay and Pinot Noir are produced annually.

TREFETHEN VINEYARDS 3 mi N of Napa off SR 29 at 1160 Oak Knoll Av PO Box 2460), Napa 94558. (707) 255-7700. Open daily 10 am to 4:30 pm for tasting. Tours by appointment. (See CSAA *Sonoma and Napa Counties* map, G-13.)

The Trefethen family took over this massive redwood winery in 1968 and put it to work after years of idleness. Surrounding the building are 600 acres of vines, from which the Trefethens make their premium varietal wines: Chardonnay, Riesling and Cabernet Sauvignon. Two proprietary blends are also vinified in the historic three-floored structure. The vineyards and production facilities can be seen by appointment.

Winery Open For Tasting Only

The following winery in the Napa area have tasting rooms on the premises but do not offer tours.

CARNEROS CREEK WINERY 1285 Dealy Ln, Napa 94559. (707) 253-9463. Open daily 9 am to 4:30 pm except major holidays. $2.50 tasting fee refundable with purchase. (See CSAA *Sonoma and Napa Counties* map, H-12.)

YOUNTVILLE AREA

S. ANDERSON VINEYARD 1473 Yountville Cross Road, Napa 94599. (707) 944-8642. Open daily 11 am to 5 pm for tasting. Tours daily at 10:30 am and 2:30 pm. (See CSAA *Sonoma and Napa Counties* map, F-13.)

After establishing their vineyard in the early 1970s and experimenting for several seasons as home winemakers, the Andersons crushed their first commercial vintage in 1979. Their 48-acre estate in the Stags Leap district produces the fruit for Chardonnay table wine and méthode champenoise sparkling wines. Tours include a visit to the 7000-square-foot cave where the sparkling wines are produced and aged.

CHATEAU CHEVRE 1 mi S of Yountville off SR 29 at 2030 Hoffman Ln, Yountville 94599. (707) 944-2184. Tours by appointment. (See CSAA *Sonoma and Napa Counties* map, F-12.)

This bucolic winery was founded in 1979 on the site of a former goat ranch, and the winery building itself originally served as the goat milking barn. The eight-and-a-half-acre vineyard was planted to Merlot in 1973, and today it supplies Merlot and Chardonnay grapes for the winery's 2000 cases of wine per year.

COSENTINO WINERY 100 yds S of Yount Hill Rd at 7415 St Helena Hwy (SR 29; PO Box 2818), Yountville 94599. (707) 944-1220. Open 10-5:30 daily for tasting; $2 tasting fee includes souvenir glass and is refundable with purchase. Tours by appointment. (See CSAA *Sonoma and Napa Counties* map, F-12.)

Mitch Cosentino custom-crushed his first wine in 1980, but it took ten years to move from his promising beginnings to his new winery in the Napa Valley, which he designed in 1985. Cosentino produces Meritage (red and white wines from the traditional Bordeaux grape varieties) as well as Cabernet Sauvignon, Cabernet Franc, Chardonnay and Merlot; Pinot Noir, a port and a dessert wine are sold only at the winery.

DOMAINE CHANDON In Yountville just W of SR 29 off California Dr (PO Box 2470), Yountville 94599. (707) 944-2280. Open daily for tasting 11 am to 6 pm May through Oct, 11 am to 6 pm Wed through Sun rest of year; $3 to $5 tasting fee per glass. Tours 11 am to 5 pm every hour on the hour. (See CSAA *Sonoma and Napa Counties* map, F-12.)

Domaine Chandon is a subsidiary of Moët-Hennessy Louis Vuitton of France, a prestigious producer of luxury items. They established this facility in 1973 and now make five styles of California sparkling wine by the traditional méthode champenoise. On a 45-minute tour, visitors to the winery will learn about all phases of this process, from tirage and aging to riddling and disgorging. Adjacent to the tasting salon is the winery's restaurant, which serves lunch and dinner; phone (800) 944-2892 for reservations.

LAKESPRING WINERY 2 mi S of Yountville at 2055 Hoffman Ln, Napa 94558. (707) 944-2475. Open weekdays 10 am to 3:30 pm for tasting. Tours by appointment. (See CSAA *Sonoma and Napa Counties* map, F-12.)

Lakespring Winery was built in 1980 by the Battat brothers as a natural expansion of their international food business. 20,000 cases of Cabernet Sauvignon, Chardonnay, Merlot, and Sauvignon Blanc are made each year in the modern winery designed by winemaker Randy Mason. There is a small picnic area on the landscaped grounds.

PINE RIDGE WINERY 5901 Silverado Trail, Napa 94558. (707) 253-7500. Open daily 11 am to 5 pm May through Sep for tasting; to 4 pm rest of year; $3 tasting fee includes souvenir glass or is refundable with purchase. Tours by appointment. (See CSAA *Sonoma and Napa Counties* map, F-13.)

Pine Ridge is located in a small fold in the hilly Stags Leap area of the Napa Valley. Fifty acres of estate vineyards, plus 100 acres elsewhere in the valley, provide the raw materials for an annual 65,000-case output of Chardonnay, Chenin Blanc, Merlot and Cabernet Sauvignon wines. Visitors are welcome to picnic.

SHAFER VINEYARDS 75 mi S of Yountville Cross Rd at 6154 Silverado Trail, Napa 94558. (707) 944-2877. Tours weekdays by appointment. (See CSAA *Sonoma and Napa Counties* map, F-13.)

John Shafer, his wife and four children moved from Chicago to the Stags Leap District in 1972 and began the arduous task of replanting 30 acres of hillside vineyards. A winery was built in 1979 against the foothills in a small valley off the Silverado Trail. The local micro-climate was responsible for the family's decision to emphasize Cabernet Sauvignon; Chardonnay and Merlot are also produced, and the vineyards have grown to 142 acres on their estate and in the Oak Knoll area and Carneros region of the Napa Valley.

SILVERADO VINEYARDS 1 mi S of Yountville Cross Road at 6121 Silverado Trail, Napa 94558. (707) 257-1770. Open daily 11 am to 4:30 pm for tasting. Tours by appointment at 10 am daily. (See CSAA *Sonoma and Napa Counties* map, F-13.)

The Walt Disney family purchased their vineyards in the Stags Leap district in the 1970s and christened them Silverado, inspired by a short book written by Robert Louis Stevenson about his Napa Valley experiences. In 1981, the family began constructing a winery. Winemaker John Stuart produces 100,000 cases per year of Cabernet,

Chardonnay, Merlot and Sauvignon Blanc, and these wines may be sampled in the tasting room. Fine art displays change periodically in the hall leading from the tasting room to a large window overlooking the Napa Valley.

ROBERT SINSKEY VINEYARDS 300 yd S of Yountville Cross Rd at 6320 Silverado Trail, Napa 94558. (707) 944-9090. Open daily during spring, summer and fall 10 am to 4:30 pm for tasting; call for winter hours; $3 tasting fee includes souvenir glass or refund with purchase. Closed major holidays. Tours by appointment.

Dr. Robert Sinskey became intrigued by the possibilities of Pinot Noir during his partnership at Acacia Winery, and in 1983 he bought vineyards of his own. His goal is estate bottled wine from his vineyards in the Carneros and Stags Leap districts. Production is 6000 cases per year of Pinot Noir, Merlot, Chardonnay, and a Merlot-based proprietary blend. The winery is built of Napa Valley stone; the aging cellar can be seen from the redwood tasting room.

STAG'S LEAP WINE CELLARS 6 mi N of Napa at 5766 Silverado Trail, Napa 94558. (707) 944-2020. Open daily 10 am to 4 pm for tasting. Tours by appointment. (See CSAA *Sonoma and Napa Counties* map, F-13.)

Stag's Leap Wine Cellars was founded by Warren and Barbara Winiarski in 1972. The well-designed modern facility sits at the foot of its namesake, a landmark rock outcropping. Its superb reputation has supported expansion to 100,000 cases of Stag's Leap and Hawk Crest (a lighter style) wines each year. Stag's Leap Wine Cellars specializes in Cabernet Sauvignon, Riesling, Chardonnay, Merlot, Petite Sirah and Sauvignon Blanc.

Although all winemaking begins in the vineyard, tours usually focus on the winery and on processes done indoors. Here at Robert Mondavi Winery, visitors get a close look at the vines.

(Robert Mondavi Winery)

OAKVILLE AREA

GIRARD WINERY 2 mi E of Oakville at 7717 Silverado Trail (PO Box 105), Oakville 94562. (707) 944-8577. Open by appointment. (See CSAA *Sonoma and Napa Counties* map, E-12.)

The Girard family built their modern winery in 1980 and crushed their first vintage that fall. The 45-acre vineyard surrounding the winery was planted to Cabernet Sauvignon and Chardonnay in 1968, and the winery also produces Chenin Blanc and Zinfandel.

GROTH VINEYARDS & WINERY

2 mi E of SR 29 at 750 Oakville Cross Rd, Oakville 94562. (707) 944-0290. Open by appointment Tue through Sat, 10 am to 4 pm.

The Groth family purchased 164 acres of Napa Valley vineyards in 1981-82 and immediately set about making Chardonnay, Sauvignon Blanc and Cabernet Sauvignon from their own grapes. Winemaker Nils Venge now produces about 34,000 cases annually of the three varietals. The new, three-level winery in the Oakville area was completed in 1990.

ROBERT MONDAVI WINERY

Oakville at 7801 St Helena Hwy (SR 29; PO Box 106), Oakville 94562. (707) 963-9611. Open daily 9 am to 5 pm May through Oct, 10 am to 4:30 pm Nov through Apr. Tours every hour on the hour; reservations recommended. (See CSAA *Sonoma and Napa Counties* map, F-12.)

In 1966 Robert Mondavi left the Charles Krug Winery, which his family has owned since 1943, to launch his own business. Architect Cliff May was commissioned to design the graceful, mission-style building, and Robert Mondavi outfitted it with oak cooperage and modern equipment. Informative guided tours cover everything from grapevines to bottling lines. Robert Mondavi wines, including Chardonnay, Riesling, Fumé Blanc, Pinot Noir and Cabernet Sauvignon, can be sampled in the tasting room. Reserve wines may be sampled in a separate tasting room for a slight fee during the summer and Thursday through Sunday during the winter. There is an art gallery and gift shop, and during July, the winery sponsors Saturday evening concerts with wine and cheese tasting at intermission.

SILVER OAK WINE CELLARS 1
mi E of Oakville at 915 Oakville Crossroad (PO Box 414), Oakville 94562. (707) 944-8808. Open Mon through Fri 9 am to 4:30 pm; Sat 10 am to 4:30 pm; $5 tasting fee includes souvenir glass or refund with purchase. Tours by appointment weekdays at 1:30 pm. (See CSAA *Sonoma and Napa Counties* map, F-12.)

Justin Meyer and Ray Duncan founded Silver Oak Cellars in 1972 to produce only one varietal: Cabernet Sauvignon. They obtain their grapes from vineyards in the Napa and Alexander Valleys, then oak and age the product five years in the bottle before release.

VICHON WINERY 1.5 mi SW of
Oakville at 1595 Oakville Grade (PO Box 363), Oakville 94562. (707) 944-2811. Open daily 10 am to 4:30 pm for tasting. Tours by appointment. (See CSAA *Sonoma and Napa Counties* map, F-12.)

This winery owned by the Robert Mondavi family sits on a leveled site high on the Oakville Grade. The modern 55,000-case-per-year facility is the source of four wines: Cabernet Sauvignon, Merlot, Chardonnay and a proprietary blend of Sauvignon Blanc and Semillon. There is a picnic area and gift shop.

VILLA MT. EDEN WINERY 2 mi E
of Oakville at 620 Oakville Crossroad (PO Box 350), Oakville 94562. (707) 944-2414. Open daily 10 am to 4 pm for tasting. Tours by appointment. (See CSAA *Sonoma and Napa Counties* map, E-12.)

The Villa Mt. Eden property began producing wine in the 1880s. It was acquired by the McWilliams family in 1969, and they subsequently added Cabernet Sauvignon and Chardonnay to the existing vineyards. Today, the winery produces about 120,000 cases per year of Cabernet Sauvignon, Chardonnay, Merlot, Pinot Noir and Zinfandel.

Winery Open For Tasting Only
The following winery in the Oakville area has a tasting room on the premises but does not offer tours.

DE MOOR WINERY 2 mi N of
Yountville at 7481 SR 29 (PO Box 348), Oakville 94562. (707) 944-2565. Open daily 10:30 to 5:30 pm in summer, 10 am to 5 pm rest of year. $1.50 tasting fee includes souvenir glass; picnic facilities available. (See CSAA *Sonoma and Napa Counties* map, F-12.)

RUTHERFORD AREA
BEAULIEU VINEYARD In Rutherford at 1960 St Helena Hwy (SR 29), Rutherford 94573. (707) 963-2411. Open daily 10 am to 5 pm. Last tour at 4 pm. (See CSAA *Sonoma and Napa Counties* map, E-12.)

Beaulieu Vineyard (also known simply as BV) is one of Napa Valley's old family wineries; it was founded in 1900 by Georges de Latour. In 1969, ownership passed to the Heublein Corporation. All of Beaulieu's table and sparkling wines are vintage-dated. Visitors to the ivy-covered building are given complete guided tours accompanied by wine tasting. In a tasting room across the parking lot from the visitors center, older vintages may be tasted for a small fee.

CAKEBREAD CELLARS 1 mi S of Rutherford at 8300 St Helena Hwy (SR 29; PO Box 216), Rutherford 94573. (707) 963-5221. Open daily 10 am to 4 pm for retail sales. Tours and tasting by appointment. (See CSAA *Sonoma and Napa Counties* map, F-12.)

This small family winery was established in 1973. The initial redwood building and a newer barrel aging facility are bordered by 73 acres of vines. The Cakebread label appears on three varietal wines: Chardonnay, Sauvignon Blanc and Cabernet Sauvignon.

CONN CREEK WINERY just S of Rutherford Cross Road at 8711 Silverado Trail, St Helena 94574. (707) 963-5133. Open 10 am to 4 pm daily for tasting. Tours by appointment. (See CSAA *Sonoma and Napa Counties* map, E-12.)

Conn Creek spent its first five years in a leased, century-old stone building north of St. Helena. In 1979 a new, energy-efficient winery was built of steel, styrofoam and gunite on the Silverado Trail. The owners concentrate on Cabernet Sauvignon, Merlot and a Meritage blend from grapes grown in vineyards at Yountville and near St. Helena.

FRANCISCAN VINEYARDS 1 mi N of Rutherford at jct of SR 29 and Galleron Rd (PO Box 407), Rutherford 94573. (707) 963-4117. Open daily 10 am to 4:30 pm for tasting; $2 tasting fee on weekends includes souvenir glass. Tours every hour beginning at 11 am with last tour at 4. (See CSAA *Sonoma and Napa Counties* map, E-12.)

Franciscan welcomes the newcomer to wine while it offers the more experienced explorer well-lit white tasting bars and a non-smoking environment. The 30-minute guided tours begin in the vineyard and cover all aspects of winemaking. Once or twice daily, visitors can learn how to assess aroma, color and other facets of wine during an introduction to sensory evaluation, and vertical tastings are conducted weekends. Franciscan is part of an estate group that produces premium varietal wine from select regions of Napa, Sonoma and Monterey counties, and Chile. And if you've always wanted to sit on the "Rutherford Bench," you can do so on the user-friendly sculpture that stands in front of the winery.

GRGICH HILLS CELLAR Rutherford at 1829 St Helena Hwy (PO Box 450), Rutherford 94573. (707) 963-2784. Open daily 9:30 am to 4:30 pm for tasting. Tours by appointment. (See CSAA *Sonoma and Napa Counties* map, E-12.)

Miljenko "Mike" Grgich has been making wine in the Napa Valley since 1958; in 1977 he and his partner, Austin Hills, built this winery. Production is about 60,000 cases per year. The emphasis has always been on Chardonnay, but Grgich also produces Sauvignon Blanc, Cabernet Sauvignon and Zinfandel.

INGLENOOK-NAPA VALLEY In Rutherford at 1991 St Helena Hwy S (SR 29; PO Box 402), Rutherford 94573. (707) 967-3363. Open daily 10 am to 5 pm for tasting. Tours every hour on the hour with the last tour at 4 pm. Closed major holidays. (See CSAA *Sonoma and Napa Counties* map, E-12.)

Inglenook's ivy-covered stone winery has been a Napa Valley landmark for decades. A family business from its establishment in 1879 until 1964, the winery is now one of the properties of the Heublein Fine Wine Group. Although the winemaking is conducted in more modern buildings, the original winery serves as a visitor center. Inglenook produces vintage-dated, estate-bottled varietals. Tasting is part of the guided tours that are given daily, and older vintages may be tasted for a fee in the John Daniel Cellar.

MUMM NAPA VALLEY 2 mi N of Oakville Cross Rd at 8445 Silverado Trail (PO Drawer 500, Rutherford 94573), Napa 94558. (707) 942-3434. Open daily 10 am to 5 pm Nov 1 through Apr 1; 10:30 am to 6 pm rest of year; $3.50 to $7.50 tasting fee includes several wines. Tours every hour on the hour with last tour at 3 pm winter, 4 pm rest of year. (See CSAA *Sonoma and Napa Counties* map, E-12.)

This méthode champenoise sparkling wine facility is the final result of a project begun in 1979 by Champagne Mumm et Cie. and Joseph E. Seagram & Sons. Tours are given daily every hour on the half hour with the last tour at 4:30 p.m. A gift shop sells wine and wine-related items.

NICHELINI VINE-YARD 11 mi E of Rutherford at jct of SR 128 and Lower Chiles Valley Rd, 2950 Sage Canyon Rd, St Helena, CA 94574. (707) 963-0717. Open weekends 10 am to 6 pm for tasting and self-guided tours. (See CSAA *Sonoma and Napa Counties* map, E-13.)

Nichelini Vineyard was founded in 1890 by Swiss-Italian immigrant Anton Nichelini. Today, four of his grandchildren own and operate the winery he built, making Cabernet, Chenin Blanc, Petite Sirah, Sauvignon Blanc and Zinfandel. Visitors are welcome to picnic under the 80-year-old walnut trees.

PEJU PROVINCE 8466 St Helena Hwy (PO Box 478), Rutherford 94573. (707) 963-3600. Open daily 10 am to 6 pm for tasting and self-guided tours; $2 tasting fee refundable with purchase. (See CSAA *Sonoma and Napa Counties* map, E-12.)

Anthony Peju crushed his first vintage in 1982, and he now produces 8000 cases per year of estate Cabernet Sauvignon, Chardonnay, French Colombard, a late-harvest Sauvignon Blanc, and a proprietary blend. The new winery, the

A wishing well lies at the center of the extensive rock and flower garden that welcomes visitors to Peju Province Winery.

Michelle De Lucie

design for which was the result of a competition between four leading California architects, opened for self-guided tours in 1991. A stone walkway leads through a flower garden, designed by Herta Peju, past a wishing well to the winery, and a number of wine-related books and gifts are available in the gift shop.

ROUND HILL WINERY 1680 Silverado Trail, St Helena 94574. (707) 963-9503, 963-5251. Open daily 10 am to 4:30 pm for retail sales. Tours by appointment. (See CSAA *Sonoma and Napa Counties* map, E-12.)

The Round Hill winery, a stockholder-owned operation, began in 1977 and moved into their present facility a decade later. Wines are produced from grapes grown in owners' vineyards and at other selected sites. At present, Round Hill makes about 300,000 cases annually of Cabernet Sauvignon, Chardonnay, Gewürztraminer, Merlot, Sauvignon Blanc and Zinfandel.

RUTHERFORD HILL WINERY 3 mi E of Rutherford off Silverado Trail at end of Rutherford Hill Rd (PO Box 410), St Helena 94574. (707) 963-7194. Open weekdays 10 am to 4:30 pm for tasting, to 5 pm weekends. Tours daily at 11:30 am, 1:30 and 3:30 pm with 12:30 and 2:30 pm tours added on weekends. (See CSAA *Sonoma and Napa Counties* map, E-12.)

This striking building, located on a wooded slope overlooking the Napa Valley, was originally constructed in 1972 to house Souverain Winery. The 60,000 square feet of constructed aging caves, which naturally regulate temperature and humidity, may be seen on tours. Rutherford Hill currently produces about 110,000 cases per year of five varietals. Tours include a visit to the caves. The visitors center contains a tasting bar and gift shop where gourmet and wine-related items are sold, and outdoor picnic tables are shaded by oak and olive trees.

ST. SUPÉRY VINEYARDS & WINERY 8440 St Helena Hwy, Rutherford 94573. (707) 963-4507. Open daily 9:30 am to 4:30 pm for tasting and tours; $2.50 tasting fee. Closed major holidays. (See CSAA *Sonoma and Napa Counties* map, F-12.)

French businessman Robert Skalli purchased the Dollarhide Ranch in Pope Valley in 1982, and in 1986 acquired property in the "Rutherford Bench" area of Napa Valley. Visitors may take a guided tour of the winery, which includes a walk through the 1882 Atkinson house, or they may follow a path through the winery for a self-guided tour. Exhibits include a topographic relief map of the Napa Valley and a smelling station where visitors can learn about wine-tasting terminology. An exhibition vineyard displays different trellising and pruning styles. Guided tours depart every fifteen minutes on weekends; on weekdays, visitors should call ahead.

SEQUOIA GROVE VINEYARDS 1 mi S of Rutherford at 8338 St Helena Hwy (SR 29), Napa 94558. (707) 944-2945. Open daily 11 am to 5 pm for tasting and self-guided tours; $3 tasting fee includes souvenir glass. (See CSAA *Sonoma and Napa Counties* map, F-12.)

Sequoia Grove's name is derived from several massive redwood trees—seemingly out of place on the Napa Valley floor—which tower over the winery. The latter is housed in a venerable barn which was reconditioned in 1980. The Allen family produces 25,000 cases each year of Chardonnay and Cabernet Sauvignon from grapes grown on the 24-acre vineyard surrounding the winery.

SULLIVAN VINEYARDS WINERY 1 mi N of Rutherford at 1090 Galleron Rd (PO Box G), Rutherford 94573. (707) 963-9646. Open daily by appointment. (See CSAA *Sonoma and Napa Counties* map, E-12.)

The Sullivan winery and residence are housed in attractive two-story wood frame buildings in the center of the Napa Valley. The first crush of Chenin Blanc and Cabernet Sauvignon grapes occurred in 1981; Merlot joined the list in 1982, and the winery also produces a red Meritage blend. All wines are big and unfined, vinified from grapes grown on the estate.

Wineries Open For Tasting Only

The following wineries in the Rutherford area have tasting rooms on the premises but do not offer tours.

CAYMUS VINEYARDS 2.5 mi E of Rutherford at 8700 Conn Creek Rd (PO Box 268), Rutherford 94573. (707) 967-3011. Open daily 10 am to 4 pm. $2 tasting fee includes souvenir glass.(See CSAA *Sonoma and Napa Counties* map, E-12.)

RUTHERFORD VINTNERS 1 mi N of Rutherford at 1673 St Helena Hwy (SR 29; PO Box 238), Rutherford 94573. (707) 963-4117. Open daily 10 am to 4:30 pm. (See CSAA *Sonoma and Napa Counties* map, E-12.)

ZD WINES 8383 Silverado Trail, Napa 94558. (707) 963-5188. Open daily 10 am to 4:30 pm. $3 tasting fee includes souvenir glass or refund with purchase. (See CSAA *Sonoma and Napa Counties* map, E-12.)

St. Helena Area

BERINGER VINEYARDS 2000 Main St, St Helena 94574. (707) 963-7115. Open daily 9:30 am to 6 pm

Visitors to Beringer Vineyards may join one of the comprehensive tours that progress from the production area to the beautiful gardens and the Rhine House.

Michelle De Lude

May 1 to Oct 30, last tour at 5 pm; open until 6 pm with last tour at 5 pm the rest of the year. Free tasting included with tour; reserve wines can be tasted upstairs for a fee without tour. (See CSAA *Sonoma and Napa Counties* map, E-11.)

Established in 1876 by the Beringer brothers, this is the oldest continuously operating winery in the Napa Valley. The Beringer home, a richly decorated 17-room mansion called the Rhine House, is listed on the National Register of Historic Places and was modeled after the family's ancestral home in Germany. Behind it, caves carved out over 100 years ago hold barrels of aging wine. These are viewed on informative 30-minute guided tours, which end at the tasting room in the Rhine House.

BUEHLER VINEYARDS 7 mi E of St Helena off Silverado Trail via Howell Mountain and Conn Valley Rds at 820 Greenfield Rd, St Helena 94574. (707) 963-2155. Tours weekdays by appointment; no tasting. (See CSAA *Sonoma and Napa Counties* map, E-12.)

The stately buildings of the Buehler family winery are situated on a wooded hillside overlooking Lake Hennessey. The 61 acres of nearby 15-year-old vineyards yield the ingredients for 30,000 cases per year of Chardonnay, Cabernet Sauvignon, Pinot Noir and red and white Zinfandel.

BURGESS CELLARS 5 mi NE of St Helena at 1108 Deer Park Rd (PO Box 282), St Helena 94574. (707) 963-4766. Open daily 10 am to 4 pm for retail sales. Tours and tasting by appointment. (See CSAA *Sonoma and Napa Counties* map, D-11.)

1972 Thomas Burgess acquired this picturesque, century-old stone winery. Its hillside location above the vineyards offers a magnificent view of the Napa Valley. Production is limited to a small selection of premium varietal table wines; the quantity is not sufficient to permit regular tasting, but by appointment visitors can arrange a tasting and tour the old aging cellars and the adjoining modern building.

CAIN CELLARS 6 mi E of St Helena at 3800 Langtry Rd, St Helena 94574. (707) 963-1616. Open by appointment for tasting and tours. (See CSAA *Sonoma and Napa Counties* map, E-10.)

Jim and Nancy Meadlock bought this winery in the Mayacamas Mountains, which was founded by the Cain family in the early 1980s. Some 100 acres of steep terraces are planted to the five Bordeaux varieties: Cabernet Sauvignon, Merlot, Cabernet Franc, Malbec and Petit Verdot, from which the winery produces two Bordeaux-style proprietary blends. Tasting and tours are offered by appointment.

THE CHRISTIAN BROTHERS GREYSTONE CELLARS 2555 Main St, St Helena 94574. (707) 967-3112. Open weekends 10 am to 4:30 pm. (See CSAA *Sonoma and Napa Counties* map, E-11.)

Greystone Cellars has stood in the Napa Valley for more than a century: construction began in June 1888 and the cellars opened 14 months later. It served as a cooperative winery for many years and was purchased by the Christian Brothers in 1950. Now it is owned by the New York-based Culinary Institute of American, which plans to install a cooking school and restaurant on the premises. Former owner Heublein, Inc., continues to run the tasting room and offers regularly scheduled tours that last about 40 minutes.

FLORA SPRINGS WINE COMPANY 1.5 mi S of St. Helena at 1978 W Zinfandel Ln, St Helena 94574. (707) 963-5711. Open by appointment Mon through Sat for tasting and tours. (See CSAA *Sonoma and Napa Counties* map, E-11.)

The fieldstone winery structure at Flora Springs was built during the late 19th century; after Prohibition, it served for a time as a cellar for Louis M. Martini's wines, and in 1977 the Komes and Garvey families bought the property. Some 400 acres produce about 2000 tons of grapes each year, with about 30% of the crop selected for Flora Springs premium wines. The winery specializes in Cabernet Sauvignon, Chardonnay, Merlot, Sauvignon Blanc and a proprietary Bordeaux-style claret for an annual output of about 40,000 cases per year. Tours may include a walk through the winery and cellar, plus tasting. A one-hour vineyard stroll is available by special request and is of special interest during the fall harvest.

FREEMARK ABBEY WINERY 2 mi N of St Helena on SR 29; PO Box 410, St Helena 94574. (707) 963-9694. Open weekdays 11 am to 5:30 pm, weekends 10 am to 5:30 for tasting; $5 fee includes souvenir glass. Tours at 2 pm daily. (See CSAA *Sonoma and Napa Counties* map, E-11.)

The stone building occupied by the winery dates back to 1895, but Freemark Abbey itself was established in 1967, when new owners acquired the property in 1967 and began a program of modernization and expansion. Now producing 38,000 cases a year, Freemark Abbey concentrates on four varietal wines: Cabernet Sauvignon, Chardonnay, Merlot and Riesling. The tasting room fireplace is lit in winter, and in spring and summer, visitors may enjoy the garden terrace.

FROG'S LEAP WINERY 3 mi N of St Helena off SR 29. (707) 963-4704. Open Mon through Fri by appointment for tasting and tours. (See CSAA *Sonoma and Napa Counties* map, D-11.)

The "Frog Farm" was once exactly that: a turn-of-the-century source of amphibians (at 33¢ a dozen) for gourmet diners. Today a converted livery stable on the creekside property is the source of premium Cabernet Sauvignon, Chardonnay, Sauvignon Blanc and Zinfandel wines, with Merlot added in 1992, made from estate-grown and purchased Napa Valley grapes. Frog's Leap schedules one tour per day, so visitors should call in advance for arrangements to tour the winery and taste the wines in an informal setting.

ROBERT KEENAN WINERY 4 mi NW of St Helena at 3660 Spring Mountain Rd, St Helena 94574. (707) 963-9177. Open by appointment for tasting and tours. (See CSAA *Sonoma and Napa Counties* map, E-11.)

This winery dates back to 1904, but when it was purchased by Robert Keenan in 1974, the vineyards had reverted to forest and only the stone walls of the original structure were still standing. The building has been handsomely restored and outfitted with new oak barrels. Production is limited to Chardonnay, Merlot, Cabernet Sauvignon and a limited production of Cabernet Franc. Visitors can make an appointment for a guided tour and tasting.

CHARLES KRUG WINERY in St. Helena at 2800 Main St, St Helena 94574. (707) 963-5057. Open daily 10 am to 5 pm; $3 tasting fee charged daily except Wed and includes souvenir glass. Tours daily except Wed at 11:30 am, 1:30 and 3:30 pm. (See CSAA *Sonoma and Napa Counties* map, E-11.)

Charles Krug founded his winery in 1861, only to have it destroyed by fire a decade later. Krug's second attempt, completed in 1874, fared better; the massive stone building he constructed is still the heart of the winery. An additional bottling and warehouse facility was added by the Peter Mondavi family, who acquired the property in 1943 and still own and operate it. The Charles Krug label now appears on a wide variety of wines, including Cabernet Sauvignon, Chardonnay, Chenin Blanc, Gamay Beaujolais, Pinot Noir and Sauvignon Blanc.

LONG VINEYARDS PO Box 50, St Helena 94574. (707) 963-2496. Tours by appointment; no tasting. (See CSAA *Sonoma and Napa Counties* map, E-12.)

The 20 acres of terraced vineyards, period buildings and modern winery that constitute this 15-year-old enterprise are situated high on a slope of Pritchard Hill above Lake Hennessey. Soil, climate and human care combine to produce exceptional grapes which are carefully vinified into less than 3500 cases of Chardonnay, Sauvignon Blanc, Riesling and Cabernet Sauvignon annually. The small output precludes tasting, but those interested in seeing a small premium operation can write Sandy Belcher for an appointment and directions.

LOUIS M. MARTINI 1 mi S of St Helena at 254 St Helena Hwy S (SR 29; PO Box 112), St Helena 94574. (707) 963-2736. Open daily 10 am to 4:30 pm for tasting; $5 tasting fee charged only for reserve wines and includes souvenir glass. Tours daily. (See CSAA *Sonoma and Napa Counties* map, E-11.)

Louis M. Martini built his winery in 1933; now, the third generation of Martinis preside over operations at the unadorned, massive building. More than 75 percent of the wine comes from the 1000 acres of Martini vineyards in the Mayacamas Mountains, Napa/Carneros area and other regions, and the grapes are brought here for crushing, fermenting and aging in the vast assortment of wood cooperage. Martini makes three lines of a large number of varietal wines.

MERRYVALE VINEYARDS at SUNNY ST. HELENA WINERY 1000 Main St, St Helena 94574. (707) 963-7777. Open daily 10 am to 5:30 pm for tasting; $3 fee refundable with purchase. Tours by appointment. (See CSAA *Sonoma and Napa Counties* map, E-11.)

After Prohibition was repealed in 1933, the St. Helena Winery was the first to be built in the Napa Valley. It produced bulk wine for many years until Christian Brothers purchased it as a storage facility in 1981; in 1986, three partners bought it for their three-year-old enterprise, Merryvale Vineyards. Today, the winery produces more than 20,000 cases per year of varietals wines.

NAPA CREEK WINERY 1001 Silverado Trail, St Helena 94574. (707) 963-9456. Open daily 10 am to 4:30 pm. (See CSAA *Sonoma and Napa Counties* map, E-12.)

Napa Creek Winery was established in 1980 in the insulated former quarters of the Sunshine Meat Packing plant. The winery now produces 12,000 cases per year of Chardonnay and Merlot from grapes purchased from Napa Valley growers. The sales room is open daily and visitors can arrange a short tour and taste the wines.

NEWTON VINEYARD 2555 Madrona Av (PO Box 540), St Helena 94574. (707) 963-9000. Tours

Friday by appointment; no tasting. (See CSAA *Sonoma and Napa Counties* map, E-11.)

Thirteen years after he founded Sterling Vineyards, Peter Newton sold that operation and turned his attention toward a new challenge. The winery that now bears his name stands amidst 560 acres of spectacularly terraced vineyards on the steep slopes of Spring Mountain above St. Helena. The winery produces Chardonnay, Cabernet Sauvignon and Merlot in the modern underground cellars and cave.

JOSEPH PHELPS VINEYARDS 2 mi SE of St Helena off Silverado Trail at 200 Taplin Rd (PO Box 1031), St Helena 94574. (707) 963-2745. Open daily 9 am to 4 pm for tasting. Tours by appointment. (See CSAA *Sonoma and Napa Counties* map, E-12.)

Joseph Phelps purchased the 670-acre Connolly ranch in 1973 following a successful career heading the nationally prominent construction company he founded 20 years earlier. The massive wood structure is designed to blend with the rolling hills and vineyards that surround it. Phelps produces 100,000 cases annually of respected red and white varietals, including Cabernet Sauvignon, Chardonnay, Johannisberg Riesling, Gewürztraminer, Merlot, Sauvignon Blanc, Scheurebe, Syrah and Viognier.

PRAGER WINERY 1.5 mi S of St Helena at 1281 Lewelling Ln, St Helena 94574. (707) 963-3720. Open daily 10 am to 4:30 pm for tasting and sales. Tours by appointment. (See CSAA *Sonoma and Napa Counties* map, E-11.)

Jim Prager and his family crushed their first vintage in 1980. The fermentation and press room is located in a century-old carriage house, while a similar new facility houses the barrel aging cellar and tasting room. Prager vinifies atypical medium-dry ports, along with Cabernet Sauvignon and Chardonnay varietals. Visitors who call ahead will begiven a tour of the small, self-contained winery by its owner.

RAYMOND VINEYARD AND CELLAR 849 Zinfandel Ln, St Helena 94574. (707) 963-8511. Open daily 10 am to 4 pm for tasting. Tours by appointment. (See CSAA *Sonoma and Napa Counties* map, E-12.)

The Raymonds launched this family enterprise in 1971 with the purchase of a 90-acre estate. Intending to produce only estate-bottled wines, they waited three years for their first crush. A winery building completed in 1978 now houses most operations. Production is currently 130,000 cases per year of Chardonnay, Cabernet Sauvignon and Sauvignon Blanc.

ST. CLEMENT VINEYARDS 1.5 mi N of St Helena at 2867 N St Helena Hwy (PO Box 261), St Helena 94574. (707) 963-7221. Open daily 10 am to 4 pm for tasting; $2 fee refundable with purchase. Tours by appointment. Closed major holidays.

The gabled Victorian house at the base of Spring Mountain was built by stained-glass merchant Fritz H. Rosenbaum in 1878. The estate was the eighth bonded winery in Napa Valley. Dr. William Casey bought the property in 1979 and built a modern winery which was sold to Sapporo Ltd. in 1987. Winemaker Dennis Johns has been at St. Clement since 1980, and current releases include Merlot, Cabernet Sauvignon, Sauvignon Blanc and Chardonnay.

SMITH-MADRONE VINEYARDS 6 mi NW of St Helena at 4022 Spring

Mountain Rd, St Helena 94574. (707) 963-2283. Open by appointment for tasting and tours. (See CSAA *Sonoma and Napa Counties* map, E-10.)

The first Smith-Madrone vines were planted in 1972, and the winery was completed six years later. The vineyards now cover about 40 acres and yield nearly 5000 cases of premium wine a year. Chardonnay and Riesling were the first varietals produced; Cabernet Sauvignon joined these beginning with the 1979 harvest. By advance arrangement, winemakers Stuart and Charles Smith will give visitors a complete overview of winery operations.

STONY HILL VINEYARD PO Box 308, St Helena 94574. (707) 963-2636. Tours by appointment; no tasting.

Perched on a crest of the Mayacamas Mountains above St. Helena is one of the smallest and most prestigious wineries in the Napa Valley. Stony Hill was bonded in 1951, when Fred McCrea began making his estate-bottled varietals in extremely limited quantities. Now winemaker Michael Chelini carries on the tradition. The Stony Hill label appears on three premium white wines—Riesling, Gewürztraminer and Chardonnay—which are sold out as soon as they are released.

TUDAL WINERY 4 mi NW of St Helena at 1015 Big Tree Rd, St Helena 94574. (707) 963-3947. Open by appointment for tasting and tours. (See CSAA *Sonoma and Napa Counties* map, D-11.)

Arnold and Alma Tudal and their family planted 10 acres of Cabernet Sauvignon vines on their property in 1974, and five years later began vinifying the yields. Only 2000 cases per year are produced from their estate.

Wineries Open For Tasting Only

The following wineries in the St. Helena area have tasting rooms on the premises but do not offer tours.

FOLIE A DEUX WINERY 2 mi N of St Helena at 3070 SR 29, St Helena 94574. (707) 963-1160. Open daily 11 am to 5 pm. (See CSAA *Sonoma and Napa Counties* map, E-11.)

HEITZ WINE CELLARS 2.5 mi S of St Helena at 436 St Helena Hwy S, St Helena 94574. (707) 963-3542. Open daily 11 am to 4:30 pm, closed major holidays. (See CSAA *Sonoma and Napa Counties* map, E-11.)

MARKHAM VINEYARDS 2812 N St Helena Hwy (PO Box 636), St Helena 94574. (707) 963-5292. Open daily 10 am to 5 pm. Gift shop. (See CSAA *Sonoma and Napa Counties* map, E-11.)

V. SATTUI WINERY 2 mi S of St Helena on SR 29 at 1111 White Ln, St Helena 94574. (707) 963-7774. Open daily 9 am to 6 pm Mar through Oct, 9 am to 5 pm rest of the year. Deli, gift shop and picnic area. (See CSAA *Sonoma and Napa Counties* map, E-11.)

SUTTER HOME WINERY, INC. 2.5 mi S of St Helena at 277 St Helena Hwy S (SR 29; PO Box 248), St Helena 94574. (707) 963-3104. Open summer weekdays 9 am to 5 pm, to 6 pm weekends; 10 am to 4:30 pm rest of year. (See CSAA *Sonoma and Napa Counties* map, E-11.)

CALISTOGA AREA

CHATEAU MONTELENA 1429 Tubbs Ln, Calistoga 94515. (707) 942-5105. Open daily 10 am to 4 pm for tasting; $5 fee refundable with purchase. Tours by appointment at 11 am

V. Sattui Winery

Some visitors to the Napa Valley find their best meal at V. Sattui Winery. The grounds are perfect for picnicking, and a wide variety of meats, cheeses and breads are available at the deli.

and 2 pm daily. Closed major holidays. (See CSAA *Sonoma and Napa Counties* map, D-10.)

Founded in 1882, Chateau Montelena was shut down during Prohibition, and production did not resume until 1972. In the meantime, former Chinese owners had added a five-acre garden lake to the property in the 1950s. Two small islands within the lake, with picnic tables shaded by green-topped pagodas, are available by reservation. The winery itself is a stone chateau carved into a hillside. Montelena specializes in four premium-quality varietals: Chardonnay, Cabernet Sauvignon, Zinfandel and Riesling.

Ladybugs are used as pest control each year in the organically farmed vineyards.

CLOS PEGASE 1 mi S of Calistoga at 1060 Dunaweal Ln (PO Box 305), Calistoga 94515. Open daily 10:30 am to 4:30 for tasting; $3 fee includes four wine samples and souvenir glass. Tours daily at 11 am and 3 pm April through October; Fri through Sun at 11 am and 3 pm rest of year.

Myth and art pervade Jan Shrem's winery. Sculptures, paintings and reliefs adorn every wall and corner from the tasting room, storage and production areas, seen on guided tours, to the winery offices, which are closed to the public. The San Francisco Museum of Modern Art sponsored the contest won by architect Michael Graves, who created two distinct façades on the southern and western sides of the facility and incorporated two Minoan columns into the architecture. The 23,000 square feet of caves hold 5000 barrels at a steady 60 degrees Fahrenheit and 90 percent humidity. The winery produces Cabernet Sauvignon, Chardonnay, Merlot, Petite Sirah and Sauvignon Blanc from more than four hundred acres of vineyards in Calistoga, St. Helena and Carneros. Slide shows scheduled for the third Saturday of each month fill up quickly; reservations should be made a month in advance.

CUVAISON 4550 Silverado Trail, Calistoga 94515. (707) 942-6266. Open daily 10 am to 5 pm for tasting. Tours by appointment only. (See CSAA *Sonoma and Napa Counties* map, D-10.)

Established in 1970, Cuvaison focuses on three varietals: Chardonnay, Cabernet Sauvignon and Merlot. All the fruit is grown on the winery's 400 acres of vineyards in the Carneros district. Visitors to the facility may picnic at the oak-shaded picnic facilities.

GUENOC WINERY 6 mi SE of Middletown at 21000 Butts Canyon Rd (PO Box 1146), Middletown 95461. (707) 987-2385. Open Thu through Sun 10 am to 4:30 pm for tasting and tours.

The Guenoc Valley was once the domain of Lillie Langtry, a popular 19th-century actress. Today her portrait graces the labels of the massive winery, which is built on a hilltop overlooking her restored ranch house. The Magoon family has planted a vineyard on 300 of their estate's 23,000 acres; production has reached 100,000 cases of wine annually. Chardonnay, Petite Sirah, Sauvignon Blanc and a red Meritage blend are among the varietal wines produced. Concerts are held periodically at the historic Langtry House, and picnickers are always welcome.

ROBERT PECOTA WINERY 2.5 mi N of Calistoga at 3299 Bennett Ln (PO Box 303), Calistoga 94515. (707) 942-6625. Open by appointment only. (See CSAA *Sonoma and Napa Counties* map, D-10.)

After a career in San Francisco as a coffee roaster and tea packer, Robert Pecota founded his own winery in 1978. North of Calistoga, on the Napa Valley floor, at the foot of Mt. St. Helena, his replanted 45-year-old vineyard is among the valley's northernmost acreage. His winery produces Sauvignon Blanc, Cabernet Sauvignon, Merlot, Gamay Beaujolais, and Muscat Blanc, and each of the three principal varietals is dedicated to one of Pecota's children. Visitors with appointments will be shown the vineyards and winery; tasting is also offered.

SCHRAMSBERG VINEYARDS 5 mi N of St Helena off SR 29; Calistoga 94515. (707) 942-4558. Tours Mon through Sat 8 am to 5 pm by appointment; no tasting. (See CSAA *Sonoma and Napa Counties* map, D-11.)

After over 100 years of sporadic operation under various owners, the Napa Valley's first hillside winery was revitalized in 1965 by its present proprietors, Jack and Jamie Davies. Schramsberg now makes five styles of méthode champenoise sparkling wines from estate-grown and purchased Napa Valley grapes. Annual production stands at about 40,000 cases.

STERLING VINEYARDS 1 mi S of Calistoga at 1111 Dunaweal Ln (PO Box 365), Calistoga 94515. (707) 942-3344. Open daily 10:30 am to 4:30 pm for tasting and self-guided tours. Closed Christmas and Thanksgiving. (See CSAA *Sonoma and Napa Counties* map, D-10.)

Sterling's first crush occurred in 1969, and the winery opened its doors in mid-1973. Production is restricted to varietal wines, which are estate bottled and vintage dated. Situated on a hilltop overlooking Napa Valley, Sterling is accessible only via an aerial tram that shuttles visitors back and forth from the parking area; the charge for the round trip is $6 per person; persons under age 16 may ride free. There is a spectacular view from the tasting room, and picnic facilities are located halfway up the tram route on Sterling Terrace.

Winery Open For Tasting Only

The following winery in the Calistoga area has a tasting room on the premises but does not offer tours.

STONEGATE WINERY 1 mi S of Calistoga at 1183 Dunaweal Ln, Calistoga 94515. (707) 942-6500. Open daily 10:30 am to 4:30 pm. Tasting $1.50 on weekends and holidays. (See CSAA *Sonoma and Napa Counties* map, D-10.)

SONOMA VALLEY AND SOUTHERN SONOMA COUNTY AREA

SONOMA

BUENA VISTA WINERY 2 mi E of Sonoma Plaza at 18000 Old Winery Rd (PO Box 1842), Sonoma, CA 95476. (800) 926-1266. Open daily 10:30 am to 5 pm for tasting. Historical presentations at 2 pm daily. (See CSAA *Sonoma and Napa Counties* map, G-12.)

Agoston Haraszthy founded Buena Vista Winery in 1857. For several years it was the largest winery in the world, but then it suffered a succession of mishaps: the vines were damaged by the plant louse phylloxera, the 1906 earthquake collapsed some of the hillside tunnels, and finally the winery closed down. Today, production is carried on in a modern winery on Buena Vista's 1300-acre estate in the Carneros district. The tasting room and art gallery are in the winery's restored press house, a State Historical Landmark, and the historical presentations last 20 to 30 minutes. Visitors are welcome to picnic in the tree-shaded picnic area.

CARMENET VINEYARD 1700 Moon Mountain Dr, Sonoma, CA 95476. (707) 996-5870. Tours by appointment only.

Carmenet is nestled in a hollow in the hills above the Sonoma Valley. Stainless steel fermentors are grouped under a unique domed, conical wooden cupola, while barrel aging takes place in four deep caverns cut into an adjacent mountain. Cabernet Sauvignon and the other red wines are made from fruit from the hilly 70-acre Moon Mountain estate vineyard; Chardonnay and Sauvignon

Blanc from the San Giacomo Vineyard in Sonoma County and the Paragon Vineyard in San Luis Obispo County's Edna Valley. Visitors who telephone ahead for an appointment will be given directions to and a tour of the winery.

CLINE CELLARS 6 mi S of Sonoma at 24737 Arnold Dr, Sonoma 95476. (707) 935-4310. Open daily 10 am to 6 pm for tasting; $1 charged only for tasting reserve or library wines. Tours weekends at 11:30 am and 3:30 pm. (see CSAA *Sonoma and Napa Counties* map.)

The emphasis at Cline Cellars is on Rhone varietals and Zinfandel. Founded in 1982, the winery moved to the Carneros district of Sonoma County in 1991, but most of the grapes still come from the family vineyards in Oakley where Cline's reputation was established; the sandy, phylloxera-resistant soil there supports vines from 40 to 100 years old. Brothers Fred and Matt Cline vinify and blend Mourvedre, Carignane, Syrah, Semillon, and Alicante bouschet for about 25,000 cases each year. More than 200 varieties of roses, ponds populated by koi, turtles and frogs, and eucalyptus shaded picnic tables provide a picturesque setting for the restored 1854 farmhouse that houses the tasting room.

GLORIA FERRER CHAMPAGNE CAVES 5 mi S of Sonoma at 23555 SR 121 (PO Box 1427), Sonoma, CA 95476. (707) 996-7256. Open daily 10:30 am to 5:30 pm for tasting; fee $2 to $4.25. Tours hourly 11 am to 4 pm. (See CSAA *Sonoma and Napa Counties* map, H-11.)

The Ferrer family is the world's largest producer of méthode champenoise sparkling wines, the best known of which is Freixenet, vinified in Cataluna in northeastern Spain. Their large Catalan-Romanesque-style winery, built in 1986, sits on a hill in the Carneros region overlooking acres of recently planted vineyards south of Sonoma. Visitors can see the underground aging caves and the other production facilities on informative tours. Tasting is available for a fee.

GUNDLACH-BUNDSCHU WINERY 2 mi E of Sonoma via Napa St and 8th St E at 2000 Denmark St, Vineburg, CA 95487. (707) 938-5277. Open daily 11 am to 4:30 pm for tasting. Tours by appointment. Closed major holidays. (See CSAA *Sonoma and Napa Counties* map, H-12.)

The partnership formed by Jacob Gundlach and Charles Bundschu in 1862 has survived for five generations, through the destruction of their entire inventory and warehouse in the 1906 San Francisco earthquake, and through Prohibition, which closed their winery. The Bundschu family remained growers until re-entering the winemaking business in the late 1960s, and today they make 50,000 cases per year of a number of varietal and two blended wines. They are the only American producers of Kleinberger (available only at the winery). Tasting is offered daily in the ivy-covered, 134-year-old winery building, which overlooks a small pond. Stone frogs, rabbits, and dwarves impart a sense of whimsy to the landscape, and a short, strenuous hike leads to a beautiful view of Sonoma Valley. The last half-mile of road to the winery is one lane wide with turnouts.

RAVENSWOOD 18701 Gehricke Rd, Sonoma, CA 95476. (707) 938-1960. Open daily 10 am to 4:30 pm for tasting. Tours by appointment.

Ravenswood winery was founded in Sonoma in 1976. Traditional methods are used in the vinification of their wines—Zinfandel, the winery's hallmark, Cabernet Sauvignon, Merlot, and a small amount of Chardonnay—from grapes grown in Napa and Sonoma counties. Production currently stands at about 40,000 cases per year. There is a small picnic area, and weekend barbecues are held during the summer on a first-come, first-served basis.

SEBASTIANI VINEYARDS in Sonoma at 389 4th St E (PO Box AA), Sonoma, CA 95476. (707) 938-5532, (800) 888-5532. Open daily 10 am to 5 pm for tasting. Tours 10:30 am to 4 pm. Closed major holidays. (See CSAA *Sonoma and Napa Counties* map, G-11.)

Sebastiani is one of California's oldest family wineries. In 1904 it produced its first wine, a Zinfandel; since then, the list has been expanded to include a full range of table and dessert wines. The winery offers tours and tasting daily and features a large collection of handcarved oak barrels. There is a gift shop, refrigerated deli items are available, and a picnic area is located adjacent to the winery.

GLEN ELLEN

ARROWOOD VINEYARDS & WINERY 1 mi N of Madrone Rd at 14347 Sonoma Hwy (SR 12; PO Box 987) Glen Ellen, CA 95442. (707) 938-5170. Open daily 10 am to 4:30 pm; tours by appointment. (See CSAA *Sonoma and Napa Counties* map, G-11.)

Sixteen years after becoming Chateau St. Jean's first winemaker—and first employee—Richard Arrowood began making wine under his own name. In 1987, he and his wife Alis built their winery (which from the road resembles a New England farmhouse) in the Valley of the Moon. Annual production is 20,000 cases of Cabernet, Chardonnay, Merlot, Viognier, and a late harvest Riesling. The tasting room is open daily,

and visitors who wish to tour the facility should make arrangements in advance.

GLEN ELLEN WINERY 1883 Jack London Ranch Rd, Glen Ellen, CA 95442. (707) 935-3000. Open daily 10 am to 4:30 pm for tasting. Tours daily at 11 am and 2 pm with additional tours at 12:30 and 3 pm summer weekends. (See CSAA *Sonoma and Napa Counties* map, G-11.)

Several generations of the Benziger family worked to transform this onetime ranch and resort into a modern wine estate. Located on the road to Jack London State Park, the winery produces a large number of varietal wines, along with several proprietary wines. The pine-paneled tasting room adjoins the cellars, and guests are welcome to picnic in the redwood grove.

MATANZAS CREEK WINERY 5 mi SE of Santa Rosa at 6097 Bennett Valley Rd, Santa Rosa, CA 95404. (707) 528-6464. Open Mon through Sat 10 am to 4 pm, Sun 12 to 4 pm for tasting and tours. (See CSAA *Sonoma and Napa Counties* map, F-10.)

Matanzas Creek Winery crushed its first vintage in the fall of 1978. Operations originally carried out in a converted dairy barn are now housed in a modern facility which was completed in 1985. The winery uses French production methods for Burgundy-style Chardonnay, Pomerol-style Merlot, and Sauvignon Blanc, which are available for tasting daily. Guests are invited to view the art on display in the Upper Barrel Room and picnic in the shade of large oaks. Groups of eight or more should call a day ahead to schedule tours.

Winery Open For Tasting Only
The following winery in the Glen Ellen area has a tasting room on the premises but does not offer tours.

VALLEY OF THE MOON WINERY

7 mi N of Sonoma at 777 Madrone Rd, Glen Ellen, CA 95442. (707) 996-6941. Open daily 10 am to 4:30 pm Jan through Mar, to 5 pm rest of year. Closed major holidays. (See CSAA *Sonoma and Napa Counties* map, G-11.)

KENWOOD

CHATEAU ST. JEAN 8 mi E of Santa Rosa at 8555 Sonoma Hwy, Kenwood, CA 95452. (707) 833-4134. Open daily 10 am to 4:30 pm for tasting; fee charged only for limited release and reserve wines. Self-guided tours daily 10:30 am to 4 pm. (See CSAA *Sonoma and Napa Counties* map, F-10.)

The founders of Chateau St. Jean purchased the 250-acre estate in 1973 and began construction of a modern winery a year and a half later. Completed in 1980, the facility is equipped with a blend of technologically advanced equipment and traditional French oak

Michelle De Lude

American novelist Jack London called Sonoma Valley "The Valley of the Moon." Nowhere are the valley's ethereal qualities more evident than here in Glen Ellen.

cooperage. St. Jean has built its renown on premium white varietals, many of which carry individual vineyard designations, and on méthode champenoise sparkling wines. Visitors may picnic on the grounds and taste the wines in the French Mediterranean mansion. Limited release and reserve wines are offered in the upstairs Vineyard Room.

KENWOOD VINEYARDS Kenwood at 9592 Sonoma Hwy (PO Box 447), Kenwood, CA 95452. (707) 833-5891. Open daily 10 am to 4:30 pm for tasting. Tours by appointment. (See CSAA *Sonoma and Napa Counties* map, F-10.)

In 1970, the Lee family bought the old Pagani Brothers bulk winery established in 1906. Since then, it has undergone a process of steady growth and modernization. Today the winery emphasizes the production of premium white and red varietal wines, including Sauvignon Blanc, Cabernet Sauvignon and Zinfandel.

LANDMARK VINEYARDS 10 mi E of Santa Rosa at jct of SR 12 and Adobe Canyon Rd; 101 Adobe Canyon Rd, Kenwood, CA 95452. (707) 833-1144. Open daily 10 am to 4:30 pm for tasting. Tours by appointment.

Bill Mabry's winemaking education began at 18 when he planted a one-quarter acre vineyard and made 80 gallons of wine in the family barn. He founded Landmark Vineyards in 1974 and built a winery in Windsor which subsequently succumbed to urban crawl. The new Kenwood winery, surrounded by Chardonnay vineyards, was completed in 1990. The early California mission-style building has a fountain in the central courtyard, and the six acres of landscaped grounds include a pond and

picnic facilities. Landmark Vineyards is California's oldest exclusively Chardonnay winery and currently produces about 20,000 cases per year.

Winery Open For Tasting Only
The following winery in Kenwood has a tasting room on the premises but does not offer tours.

ST. FRANCIS WINERY 8450 Sonoma Hwy, Kenwood, CA 95452. (707) 833-4666. Open daily 10 am to 4:30 pm. Gift shop, refrigerated deli items and picnic area. (See CSAA *Sonoma and Napa Counties* map, F-10.)

SANTA ROSA AREA

ADLER FELS 7 mi NE of Santa Rosa at 5325 Corrick Ln, Santa Rosa, CA 95409. (707) 539-3123. Tasting and tours by appointment only.

David Coleman and Ayn Ryan built their picturesque winery 1500 feet above the Sonoma Valley in 1980. They annually produce about 15,000 cases of white and red varietal table and sparkling wines from grapes purchased from selected North Coast county growers. The winery's name derives from Eagle Rock, a nearby local landmark.

FISHER VINEYARDS 6200 St Helena Rd, Santa Rosa, CA 95404. (707) 539-7511. Tours and sales by appointment; no tasting.

Located at an elevation of 1200 feet on the western slope of the Mayacamas Mountains, Fred Fisher's vineyards include plantings of Chardonnay and Cabernet Sauvignon dating from 1974. The small family winery was constructed of redwood and Douglas fir grown on the property. Interested individuals who wish to visit the facility should write or call well in advance for an appointment and directions.

Central Valley

California's most productive wine region is the San Joaquin Valley. Extremely warm summer temperatures combine with rich soil to produce a crop that nearly doubles the Napa Valley average per acre. The conditions are particularly good for the production of table and raisin grapes and dessert wines, but the valley also produces over half of California's table and sparkling wines.

Vineyards in the southern part of the San Joaquin Valley are planted largely with raisin and table grapes, such as the Thompson Seedless, but vast vineyards of wine grapes are cultivated near Bakersfield. Farther north, in Modesto, is the largest of California wineries: E. & J. Gallo. The Gallo brothers have used mass production and the valley's high grape yield to full advantage: their numerous vineyards and winemaking facilities (all closed to the public) make them perhaps the largest winery in the world. Only recently has Gallo turned its attention toward acreage in what is commonly thought of as "wine country"—the northern California coastal region—and begun phasing out the "Gallo" label. Its labels now include Sheffield, Gallo Livingston Cellars, Wycliffe and Copperidge Chardonnay.

FICKLIN VINEYARDS 30246 Av 7.5, Madera 93637. (209) 674-4598. Open weekdays by appointment for tasting and tours. (See CSAA *Yosemite* map.)

The Ficklin family has been involved in San Joaquin Valley grape growing since 1911. In the 1940s they planted four Portuguese varietals on an experimental basis, and in 1948 began making port wine exclusively from the resulting grapes. The practice has continued to the present day; now the third generation of Ficklins produces their non-vintage Tinta Port and special limited bottlings of vintage port. When time permits, winemaker Peter Ficklin will show visitors with appointments through the adobe facility.

A. NONINI WINERY 10 mi NW of Fresno via McKinley Av at 2640 N Dickenson Av, Fresno 93722. (209) 275-1936. Open Mon through Sat 9 am to 4 pm for tasting. Tours by appointment. Closed for lunch noon to 1 pm and closed major holidays.

(See CSAA *Fresno and Kings Counties* map, D-6.)

This winery has been a family business since its establishment in 1936 by Antonio and Angiolina Nonini. The Nonini wines include four styles of Zinfandel and several generic table wines; these are distributed primarily to local stores and restaurants. For guests wishing to investigate the wines, there is informal tasting.

QUADY 13181 Rd 24, Madera 93637. (209) 673-8068. Open Mon through Fri 9 am to 5 pm and weekends by appointment for tasting and tours. (See CSAA *Yosemite* map.)

Andrew Quady began making vintage port from Amador County Zinfandel grapes in 1975. His original compact winery building forms one wing of the modern concrete and stucco facility opened in 1985. Quady produces about 13,000 cases per year of premium dessert wines. The equipment includes stainless steel fermentors, an ancient

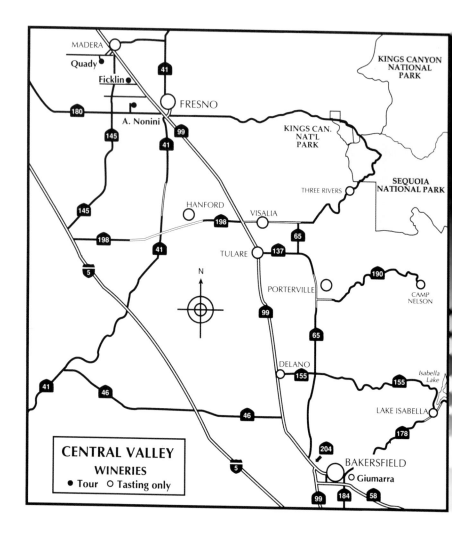

crusher and French oak barrels. Visitors are welcome to tour the premises and sample the wines.

Winery Open For Tasting Only

The following winery has a tasting room on its premises but does not offer tours.

GIUMARRA VINEYARDS 8 mi E of Bakersfield off SR 58 on Edison Hwy; PO Bin 1969, Bakersfield 93303. (805) 395-7088. Open Tue through Sat 9 am to 5 pm. (See ACSC *Kern County* map, E-12.)

Sierra Foothills

The region of rolling countryside known as the Mother Lode stretches along the western slopes of the Sierra Nevada. The first vineyards here were reputedly planted by miners during the gold rush. By 1890 there were more than a hundred foothill wineries in operation, but their prosperity was short-lived. As the gold played out, the miners moved on, and winemaking dwindled steadily until Prohibition ended it. Most of the wineries currently established in the region were founded in the 1970s although many of the buildings that house them are considerably older.

Viticulture in the foothill counties continues to expand. Although frost danger limits the amount of productive vineyard acreage, the climate is suitable for premium varietals. In fact, the high quality of the grapes has attracted distant wineries like Ridge, Carneros Creek and Sutter Home, which have helped establish the region's reputation for Zinfandel.

Another center of activity is Lodi, where a tenth of the state's wine is produced. Numerous wineries, including several cooperatives, are clustered around the town. From Lodi, the Sacramento Valley extends north nearly 200 miles. This was a thriving wine district prior to Prohibition, but only a few local wineries are now in operation.

For road coverage, members should refer to the CSAA *Lake Tahoe Region* map. Detailed information about the Gold Rush towns is contained in the Auto Club of Southern California's *Mother Lode* book.

ANNUAL EVENTS

Exact dates, prices and other information about the events listed below may be verified by calling the telephone numbers shown. Some wineries also individually sponsor special brunches, dinners and summer concerts. Those interested in the events sponsored by a particular winery should call that winery and ask if a calendar of events is available.

MARCH-APRIL—
El Dorado County Passport Weekend *various wineries and locations.* (916) 622-7221. A two-weekend event of wine tasting including library vintages, new releases, wine from the barrel, wine and food pairing, demonstrations, vineyard tours and music. A limited number

of tickets are available at $30 per weekend; order from El Dorado Winery Association, PO Box 1614, Placerville, CA 95667.

APRIL—
Lodi Spring Wine Show and Food Faire, *Lodi.* (209) 369-2771. 40 wineries and 10 restaurants provide samples of wine and food. There are also fine arts, photography and craft displays and cooking demonstrations. Call for ticket prices.

MAY—
Sierra Showcase of Wine Amador County Fairgrounds, *Plymouth.* (209) 274-4766. Tickets can be ordered in advance or purchased at the gate. Activities include a barbecue, wine,

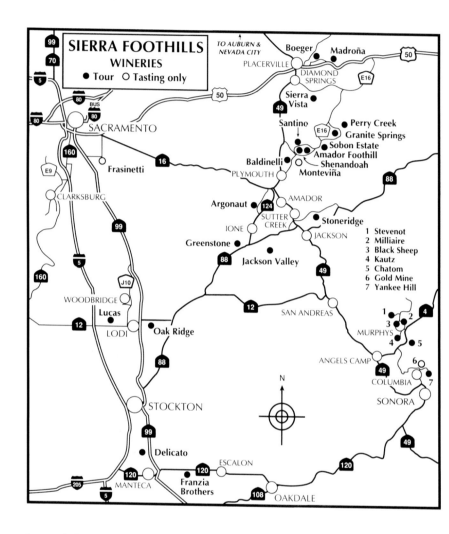

fruit and cheese tasting, art show, live music and an auction. Call for ticket prices.

JUNE—

Fairplay Wine Festival various wineries in Fairplay area of El Dorado County. (209) 245-6395. A variety of live music, wine tasting, cheeses, art exhibits, games, special discounts. Commemorative logo glass $2 or bring your own for tasting.

JULY—

Music at the Wineries Jazz Festivals various wineries in *Amador County*. (209) 267-0211. Live music, hors d'oeuvres and wine tasting.

SEPTEMBER—

Delicato Grape Stomp Lodi. (209) 825-6213. This event held on Labor Day Sunday sponsors a grape stomp, classic car show, amateur winemaking, live music, and arts and crafts displays.

Glenn Kahl

One of the highlights of September's Delicato Grape Stomp is—the grape stomp. Other events include a classic car show and amateur winemaking.

Bluegrass Concert *Murphys*, at Stevenot Winery. (209) 728-3436.

OCTOBER—

Wine Appreciation Week *Amador County*, various wineries and locations. (209) 245-4455. Grape stomp, live music, barrel tasting, art demonstrations, barbecues, food and meet-the-winemaker events.

CALIFORNIA STATE HIGHWAY 99

DELICATO VINEYARDS 4 mi N of Manteca on Hwy 99, Manteca 95336. (209) 825-6212, 239-1215. Open daily 9 am to 5:30 pm for tasting. Tours Fri at 10 am, 2 and 4 pm, and by appointment. (See CSAA *Bay and River Area* map.)

Since the first vineyards were planted in 1924, this facility has been owned and managed by the Indelicato family. Their wines bear the amended and euphonic version of the family name. A number of varietal and generic table wines are produced at the 40-million-gallon facility. Visitors can enjoy the wines in a modern, round tasting room.

THE LUCAS WINERY 2 mi W of Lodi off Turner Rd at 18196 N Davis Rd, Lodi 95242. (209) 368-2006. Open by appointment only. (See CSAA *Lake Tahoe Area* map.)

David and Tamara Lucas produce 1000 cases a year of Zinfandel from five acres of low-yielding, 65-year-old vines. Their barrel aging, storage and tasting rooms are housed in three compact buildings adjacent to their home, on a country road near Lodi. Tours provide a thorough look at a small-scale, labor-intensive family winemaking operation.

OAK RIDGE VINEYARDS 1 mi E of Lodi at 6100 E SR 12, Lodi 95240. (209) 369-4758. Open daily 9 am to 5 pm for tasting. Tours during the fall crush season. (See CSAA *Lake Tahoe Area* map.)

Oak Ridge is one of several wineries in the Lodi region owned by a growers' cooperative. Founded in 1934, it has developed a full line of table and aperitif wines. Visitors are offered a variety of samples in the tasting room, which is housed in a converted redwood aging tank, and tables are available for picnickers.

Winery Open For Tasting Only

The following winery has a tasting room on its premises but does not offer tours.

FRASINETTI WINERY 3 mi E of SR 99 at 7395 Frasinetti Rd (PO Box 28213), Sacramento 95828. (916) 383-2444. Open Tue through Sat 11 am to 9 pm, Sun until 3 pm. Restaurant on premises. (See CSAA *Lake Tahoe Area* map.)

CALAVERAS COUNTY

BLACK SHEEP VINTNERS at the W end of Main St at jct of Murphys Grade Rd (PO Box 1851), Murphys 95247. (209) 728-2157. Open weekends and holidays noon to 5 pm for tasting and tours, and by appointment. (See CSAA *Lake Tahoe Area* map.)

Janis and Dave Olson named their winery Black Sheep Vintners because, like a black sheep, they hope to be different. They released their first vintage in 1986

and have grown from 500 to 2000 cases per year. Their specialty is Zinfandel, and they also make Cabernet Sauvignon, Chardonnay and Sauvignon Blanc, all from Sierra Foothill grapes.

CHATOM VINEYARDS 8 mi E of Angels Camp at 1969 SR 4, Douglas Flat 95229. (209) 736-6500. Open daily 11 am to 4:30 pm; tours by appointment. (See CSAA *Lake Tahoe Area* map.)

Gay Callan's family has been in agriculture for several generations, but Callan's efforts began in 1981, when she planted the Esmeralda Valley vineyard, quit her job in the South Bay and returned to school to study viticulture. Chatom Vineyards wine production began in 1985 and currently stands at 5000 cases per year of Cabernet Sauvignon, Chardonnay, Sauvignon Blanc, Merlot, Semillon and Zinfandel. Visitors with appointments may tour the rammed earth winery building.

KAUTZ VINEYARDS 1 mi S of Murphys via Algiers St at 1894 Six-Mile Rd, Murphys 95247. (209) 728-1251. Open daily 11 am to 4:30 pm for tasting. Tours by appointment. (See CSAA *Lake Tahoe Area* map.)

John H. Kautz combined his experience as grower with his interest in wine on his Hay Station Ranch, once a Wells Fargo stagecoach station. He and his sons finished the first step, the man-made aging caves, in 1990. Two tunnels, each 185 feet long, connected by four 100-foot cross-tunnels, have the rough, mysterious appearance of natural caves and house a waterfall and music room. Tasting is conducted here, where the temperature remains a constant 60 degrees Fahrenheit with 75 percent humidity. In addition to Cabernet Sauvignon, Chardonnay, Merlot and Symphony, Kautz also sells apples (in season) from its 60-acre hillside orchard. There is a shaded picnic area beside a large pond. Under construction are a production and storage facility (the second floor of which will house a museum) and an outdoor amphitheater.

MILLIAIRE WINERY In Murphys at 276 Main Street (PO Box 1554), Murphys 95247. (209) 728-1658. Open daily 11 am to 4:30 pm for tasting and tours. (See CSAA *Lake Tahoe Area* map.)

Steve Millier began his winemaking career in 1975 at the David Bruce Winery in Santa Cruz. In 1982, he and his wife Elizabeth left the California coast for the Sierra Nevada mountains and moved to Murphys, where Steve worked as winemaker at Stevenot Winery until 1989. In 1983, the Milliers founded their winery ("milliaire" means "milestone" in French), which produces only 1000 cases per year of Cabernet Sauvignon, Chardonnay, Gewürztraminer, Merlot, Sauvignon Blanc, Zinfandel and several dessert wines, all from Sierra Foothills fruit. At harvest time, the crushing and pressing machines are operated in front of the old carriage house on Main Street that houses the winery. Tasting and tours are offered daily.

STEVENOT WINERY 3 mi N of Murphys on San Domingo Rd (PO Box 548), Murphys 95247. (209) 728-3436. Open daily 10 am to 5 pm for tasting. Tours by appointment. (See CSAA *Lake Tahoe Area* map.)

Stevenot is one of the most prominent family names in Mother Lode country. Owner Barden Stevenot founded the winery in 1974 on the site of the former Shaw Ranch, and many of the winery buildings date back to the turn of the century. 45,000 cases of wine per year

are produced in a restored hay barn and in a newer, similarly-styled structure. 27 acres of vineyards are planted to Cabernet Sauvignon, Chardonnay, Merlot and Zinfandel. The winery also makes two dessert wines, available only at the winery. Refrigerated deli items are sold in the rustic tasting room and gift shop, built in 1903, and picnic tables are shaded by grape arbors in a garden setting.

YANKEE HILL WINERY .75 mi E of Columbia on Yankee Hill Rd (PO Box 330), Columbia 95310. (209) 533-2417. Open daily 10 am to 6 pm for tasting. Tours upon request. (See CSAA *Lake Tahoe Area* map.)

Built in 1970, Yankee Hill Winery produces an assortment of table, sparkling and berry wines. These currently total 2500 cases a year. Vineyards are being planted, and in the meantime, grapes are purchased locally. Owner Ron Erickson and members of his family give tours upon request and pour samples of the wine. There is a deck area where visitors can sit at tables and a picnic area underneath the trees.

Wineries Open For Tasting Only

The following wineries in Calaveras County have a tasting room on the premises but do not offer tours.

GOLD MINE WINERY 5 mi S of Columbia State Park at 22265 Parrotts Ferry Rd, Sonora 95370. (209) 532-3089. Open Tue through Sun 11 am to 5 pm. (See CSAA *Lake Tahoe Area* map.)

INDIAN ROCK VINEYARD 1.5 mi SE of Murphys on Pennsylvania Gulch Rd, Murphys 95247. (209) 728-2266. Open weekends and holidays 11 am to 5 pm, or by appointment. (See CSAA *Lake Tahoe Area* map.)

AMADOR COUNTY

AMADOR FOOTHILL WINERY 6 mi NE of Plymouth off Shenandoah Rd at 12500 Steiner Rd, Plymouth 95669. (209) 245-6307. Open weekends noon to 5 pm for tasting. Informal tours upon request. (See CSAA *Lake Tahoe Area* map.)

Amador Foothill currently produces about 10,000 cases annually of white and red Zinfandel, Sangiovese and Sauvignon Blanc; all are made from locally grown grapes. Visitors can see the two-level, energy-efficient building which uses a passive rock-bed cooling system. Picnickers are welcomed.

ARGONAUT WINERY 5 mi NE of Ione via SR 124 and Willow Creek Rd at 13675 Mt Echo Dr, Ione 95640. (209) 274-4106. Open by appointment for tours and tasting. (See CSAA *Lake Tahoe Area* map.)

A partnership launched this winery in 1976. It is primarily a weekend operation, producing just 2000 cases per year. The emphasis is on three varietals: estate-grown Barbera, Syrah and Shenandoah Valley Zinfandel.

BALDINELLI VINEYARDS 4 mi NE of Plymouth via Shenandoah Rd at 10801 Dickson Rd, Plymouth 95669. (209) 245-3398. Open Sat and Sun 11 am to 4 pm for tasting and tours. (See CSAA *Lake Tahoe Area* map.)

Seventy acres of sixty-year-old Zinfandel and younger Sauvignon Blanc and Cabernet Sauvignon vines provide the basis for Ed Baldinelli's wines. The Shenandoah Valley facility was built in 1979 and now produces 17,000 cases annually.

GREENSTONE WINERY 11 mi W of Jackson at jct of SR 88 and Jackson Valley Rd at 3151 SR 88 (PO Box 1164), Ione 95640. (209) 274-2238. Open for tasting Wed through Sun 10 am to 4 pm in summer, Fri through Sun 10 am to 4 pm rest of year. Tours by appointment. (See CSAA *Lake Tahoe Area* map.)

Greenstone Winery was constructed in 1979 using local greenstone in a French-country design with a spacious lower level and high sloping ceilings. The height and shape of the building naturally creates different temperature zones for different stages of production and for aging various kinds of wine. The Fowler and Van Spanje families produce a large number of varietal wines and guide interested visitors with appointments on informative, hour-long tours. The picnic area overlooks an artificial pond.

JACKSON VALLEY VINEYARDS 6.5 mi S of Ione at 4851 Buena Vista Rd, Buena Vista/Ione 95640. (209) 274-4721. Open daily 11 am to 4 pm for tasting. Tours by appointment. (See CSAA *Lake Tahoe Area* map.)

A picturesque duck pond and sixty acres of vines frame the restored century-old barn which houses the Jackson Valley Winery. The 30,000-case annual production is made from estate-grown fruit along with purchased Zinfandel grapes. The winery is open for tasting daily and tours by appointment. Picnic facilities are available.

SANTINO WINES 5 mi NE of Plymouth via Shenandoah Rd at 12225 Steiner Rd, Plymouth 95669. (209) 245-6979. Open daily noon to 4:30 pm. Tours by appointment. (See CSAA *Lake Tahoe Area* map.)

The Santino winery began operations in 1979 in a modern Shenandoah Valley facility. Emphasis so far has been on several styles of wine vinified from the Zinfandel grape. The 30,000-case annual output also includes a late harvest Riesling, two fortified dessert wines, a blend of Portuguese port, and some Barbera and Sauvignon Blanc. Picnic facilities are available.

SHENANDOAH VINEYARDS 5 mi NE of Plymouth via Shenandoah Rd at 12300 Steiner Rd, Plymouth 95669. (209) 245-4455. Open daily 10 am to 5 pm for tasting and tours. (See CSAA *Lake Tahoe Area* map.)

Leon Sobon left his job as a research scientist to launch his own winery in 1977. With the help of his wife Shirley and six children, he produces about 30,000 cases each year. Forty-two acres of vineyard adjoin the hilltop winery; grapes are also purchased from local growers. The wine list includes four dry varietals, along with three dessert wines.

SOBON ESTATE 7 mi NE of Plymouth at 14430 Shenandoah Rd, Plymouth 95669. (209) 245-6554. Open daily 10 am to 5 pm for tasting and tours. (See CSAA *Lake Tahoe Area* map.)

Leon and Shirley Sobon celebrated their 30th wedding anniversary by opening a new winery near their Shenandoah Vineyards. Formerly the D'Agostini Winery, this historical landmark is the third oldest winery in the state, built by Adam Uhlinger in 1856. The 60 acres of adjoining vineyard are planted to Zinfandel and still contain some of the original plantings. The original cellars are still in use, and staves from six of the old redwood tanks make up one wall of the tasting room, which is housed in what was once D' Agostini's warehouse and bottling room. Early winemaking and agricultural equipment is on display in the Shenandoah Valley Museum across from the tasting room. A picnic area fronts the winery.

STONERIDGE 4 mi SE of Sutter Creek at 13862 Ridge Rd East, Sutter Creek 95685. (209) 223-1761. Open Sat and Sun noon to 4 pm or by appointment. (See CSAA *Lake Tahoe Area* map.)

StoneRidge is one of the smallest commercial wineries in the foothill region, producing less than 1500 gallons a year. Owners Gary and Loretta Porteous do all the work themselves, from pruning to bottling. Their fermenting shed and wine cellar, built in 1975, are open for tours when time allows. Visitors are also welcome to taste the two StoneRidge wines: Zinfandel and Ruby Cabernet.

Winery Open For Tasting Only
The following winery in Amador County has a tasting room on the premises but does not offer tours.

MONTEVIÑA 3 mi NE of Plymouth via Shenandoah Rd at 20680 Shenandoah School Rd, Plymouth (PO Box 100) 95669. (209) 245-6942. Open daily 11 am to 4 pm. Gift shop, art gallery, picnic area. (See CSAA *Lake Tahoe* map.)

EL DORADO COUNTY

BOEGER WINERY 5 mi N of US 50 via Schnell School Rd at 1709 Carson Rd, Placerville, CA 95667. (916) 622-8094. Open daily 10 am to 5 pm for tasting and self-guided tours. (See CSAA *Lake Tahoe Area* map.)

The Boeger Winery was established in 1973 on a ranch site that dates back to the 1870s. Some of the original stone buildings still stand, including an 1872 wine cellar in which the tasting room is located. Boeger was the first modern-day winery to locate in El Dorado county and now produces 15,000 cases per year from its 55 acres of vineyards. Varietals include Cabernet, Zinfandel, Barbera and Merlot. The picnic area is open daily.

GRANITE SPRINGS WINERY .5 mi S of Somerset off Fairplay Rd at 6060 Granite Springs Rd, Somerset 95684. (209) 245-6395 and (916) 621-1933. Open Wed through Sun 11 am to 5 pm for tasting and informal tours. (See CSAA *Lake Tahoe Area* map.)

Dug into a granite hillside, Granite Springs was founded by Les and Lynne Russell in 1981. The winery is surrounded by vineyards planted to Sauvignon Blanc, Cabernet Sauvignon, Cabernet Franc, Zinfandel and Petite Sirah. Founded in 1981, Granite Springs currently produces 12,000 cases per year of varietal wines, a vintage port and a black muscat. A picnic area is available.

MADROÑA VINEYARDS 5 mi E of Placerville off US 50 and Carson Rd through High Hill Ranch (PO Box 454), High Hill Rd, Camino 95709. (916) 644-5948. Open daily 11 am to 5 pm for tasting. Tours by appointment. (See CSAA *Lake Tahoe Area* map.)

The vineyards at Madroña—perhaps California's highest, at an elevation of 3000 feet—were planted in 1973-74, and initially the yields were sold to other wineries. In 1980, the winery was constructed, and today the winery produces Johannisberg Reisling, Gewürztraminer, Merlot, Cabernet Franc, and late harvest dessert wines among others.

PERRY CREEK VINEYARDS 16 mi S of Placerville off Mt. Aukum Rd at 7400 Perry Creek Rd (PO Box 304), Somerset 95684. (209) 245-5175.

Open weekends 11 am to 5 pm and by appointment for tasting and tours.

Michael Chazen left the textile industry where he made his fortune, tired of the international commute that had him spending half his time in the U.S. and half of it in Korea. He and his wife Alice run this state-of-the-art oasis near the middle fork of the Consumnes River. Winemaker Nancy Steel vinifies Perry Creek's complex yet accessible wines, including a dry Alsatian-style Riesling and a white Zinfandel "for people who don't like white Zinfandel." 50 acres of vineyards are planted to Nebbiolo, Sangiovese, Muscat Canelli, Syrah, Viognier, Zinfandel, Merlot and Cabernet Franc. Production is 6000 cases per year. There are plenty of picnic facilities, the gift shop stocks gourmet food items, and Chazen's collection of classic automobiles is on display.

SIERRA VISTA WINERY 12 mi SE of Placerville via Pleasant Valley Rd and Leisure Ln at 4560 Cabernet Wy, Placerville 95667. (916) 622-7221. Open weekends 11 am to 5 pm or by appointment. (See CSAA *Lake Tahoe Area* map.)

John and Barbara MacCready founded their small winery in 1977. In addition to Cabernet Sauvignon, Chardonnay and Zinfandel, attention is also focused on Syrah and other varieties of the Rhône region of France. Annual production now stands at 8000 cases. The winery is open for tasting every weekend and weekdays by appointment; visitors should pre-arrange tours.

NEVADA COUNTY

NEVADA CITY WINERY 321 Spring St, Nevada City, CA 95959. (916) 265-9463. Open daily noon to 5 pm for tasting and tours. (See CSAA *Lake Tahoe Area* map.)

An old tin garage in picturesque Nevada City houses this three-level winery founded in 1980. Grapes purchased from Nevada County vineyards account for an annual 8000-case output of varietal and generic wines. Visitors are able to observe the production area from the tasting room.

Glossary of Wine Terms

Acidity—
a term used in wine tasting to indicate agreeable sharpness or tartness produced by natural fruit acids; a good wine should have balanced acidity and sweetness.

Appellation—
the designation of a wine's geographic origin, such as the name of a particular vineyard, county or district.

Astringency—
the mouth-puckering sensation produced by tannin in wine; young wines with high astringency usually smooth out with age.

Body—
the consistency or "weight" of wine on the tongue. Red wines tend to be heavy-bodied and white wines lighter.

Botrytis cinerea—
called "noble rot," Botrytis is a unique plant mold producing concentrated sweetness and flavor in affected grapes; it plays a significant part in the production of sweet white wines in Europe and in California's coastal counties.

Bottle sickness—
a temporary decline in a wine's quality that results from agitation during bottl-ing or shipping; the wine normally recovers within a few weeks.

Bouquet—
the fragrance of a wine created by fermentation and aging, developing as the wine matures.

Brut—
a term used to describe extremely dry champagnes.

Carbonic Maceration—
a technique of fermentation employed in the production of Beaujolais-style wines in which whole grape clusters and their stems are fermented together; the grapes are usually pressed afterward to extract the wine, which is light, fruity and intended for early consumption.

Charmat (or bulk) process—
the method of producing sparkling wines in which the second fermentation is conducted in large glass-lined tanks, thereby speeding up production and lowering cost.

Clarification—
removal of sediment from aged wines before bottling by racking, fining or fil-tering.

Cooperage—
the general term used for bulk containers in which wine is aged, particularly wooden barrels and tanks.

Cuvée—
a blend of wines bottled as one lot; usually refers to the blend of still wines used to make champagnes.

Decant—
to pour wine from the bottle into a serving container so that any sediment remains in the bottle and clear wine is obtained.

Disgorge—
to remove sediment from sparkling wines by uncorking the bottle and allowing the frozen plug in the neck (where solids have settled during riddling) to escape.

Dosage—
the small amount of syrup and aged wine added to sparkling wines after disgorging; the dosage determines the sweetness of champagnes.

Enology (oenology)—
the science of wine and winemaking.

Estate bottled—
wine fermented, aged and bottled by a winery located in the viticultural area named on the wine's label and made from grapes grown in that area by the winery.

Fining—
the method of wine clarification which uses a settling agent such as egg white or gelatin to precipitate sediment.

Finish—
a wine-tasting term referring to the palate sensation or aftertaste remaining after the wine is swallowed.

Flor—
a yeast growth which develops on the surface of wines in partially filled containers, giving flor sherries their distinctive flavor.

Free-run juice—
juice that drains from grapes during crushing before the skins are squeezed in a press.

Generic—
a term applied to wines that are named after European wine-producing districts (e.g., burgundy, chablis, sauterne); generic wines also include those bearing general labels (e.g., claret, chianti, vin rosé). Usually several grape varieties are blended to make generic wines, which are generally less expensive than varietal wines.

Late harvest—
a term used to describe a wine (frequently Riesling) made from grapes picked at an advanced state of ripeness, giving the wine extra sweetness and flavor.

Legs—
the pattern produced when wine is swirled in a glass, clinging to the sides as it descends.

Méthode champenoise—
the original French method of producing champagnes in which the wine undergoes its second fermentation in the bottle; this process is costlier and more time-consuming than the Charmat process. Sparkling wines produced by the champenoise method may bear the label "naturally fermented in this bottle."

Must—
the mixture of grape juice, pulp and skin produced by crushing.

Natur (or Natural)—
a term used to describe the driest champagnes, to which no dosage has been added.

Non-vintage—
a term referring to wine bottles that aren't identified by a vintage year on the label; non-vintage wines often contain a blend of grapes from different years.

Nose—
a general term referring to the combined grape aroma and bouquet of a wine.

Organic—
made without the use of synthetic pesticides, fertilizers or other synthetic chemicals.

Oxidized—
the word used to describe wine that has had excessive exposure to air, damaging the flavor and color. Oxidation results from improper handling or storage.

Phylloxera—
a plant louse that attacks the roots of grapevines. Phylloxera was responsible for the massive destruction of European vineyards in the late 19th century; a remedy, grafting European vines (Vitis vinifera) to American rootstock (Vitis labrusca), was discovered in time to halt the destruction of California vineyards. A new type of the louse, to which currently planted rootstock is not resistant, now threatens thousands of acres of California vineyards.

Pomace—
grape skins, seeds and pulp that remain after the grapes have been crushed and the wine pressed or drawn off.

Racking—
a method of wine clarification in which clear wine is drawn from one container to another, leaving behind the deposit of sediment.

Riddling—
the process of collecting sediment in the necks of champagne bottles by placing the bottles upside-down in a special rack and turning them daily to work the deposit into the necks.

Sec—
a term used to describe still or sparkling wines that are semi-dry; literally, "dry" in French.

Sediment—
the deposit of particles that have settled in the cask or bottle during aging.

Solera—
a tier of casks used to blend sherries of different ages by drawing the oldest wine from the bottom cask for bottling and replacing it with newer wine from the casks above.

Tannin—
an acid contained in grape skins and seeds which is released during crushing and fermentation and which gives wine astringency. Because they are fermented in contact with the grape skins, red wines have a higher tannin content than white wines.

Tartrates—
clear, harmless crystals of tartaric acid that form as wine is aged; their presence is particulary common in white wine.

Transfer method—
a variation of the champenoise method of producing sparkling wine; the wine is fermented in the bottle but transferred to holding tanks for filtration, after which the wine is rebottled and the dosage added. Some wines produced by the transfer method bear the label "naturally fermented in the bottle."

Ullage—
the amount of wine lost during aging through evaporation or leakage.

Varietal—
the term applied to wines that contain at least 75 percent of the grape variety named on the label (e.g., Cabernet Sauvignon, Pinot Noir, Chardonnay); many vintners use a greater percentage in order to emphasize the characteristic flavor and aroma of the grape variety.

Vintage—
the year the grapes in a wine were harvested; a vintage date on the label indi-

cates that at least 95% of the grapes were from that year.

Vitis labrusca—
a hardy species of grapevine, including such varieties as Concord and Delaware, native to North America; used in winemaking in the eastern United States and Canada and as disease-resistant rootstock for vinifera vines.

Vitis vinifera—
the classical family of grapevines, including such premium grapes as Cabernet Sauvignon and Chardonnay, imported from Europe and particularly well suited to the gentle climate of California.

Wine thief—
a long glass tube used to extract samples of wine from the barrel.

Index of Wineries

Wineries with italicized names are open for tasting only, no tours. Page numbers in italics refer to photos.

A

A. Nonini Winery..............................91
Acacia Winery 67
Adelaida Cellars..............................28
Adler Fels 90
Alderbrook Winery 51
Alexander Valley Vineyards..............51
Amador Foothill Winery 98
Anderson Vineyard, S......................70
Arciero Winery 29
Argonaut Winery 98
Arrowood Vineyards & Winery 88
Austin Cellars 26

B

Babcock Vineyards...........................23
Baily Vineyard & Winery 18
Baldinelli Vineyards.........................98
Bargetto Winery...............................35
Beaulieu Vineyard............................74
Bellerose Vineyard 51
Belvedere Winery...........................55
Beringer Vineyards...........................78
Bernardo Winery...............................16
Black Sheep Vintners 96
Boeger Winery 99
Bonny Doon Vineyard.......................36
Brander Vineyard..............................24
Bruce Winery, David 40
Buehler Vineyards.............................79
Buena Vista Winery...........................86
Burgess Cellars 79
Bynum Winery, Davis 52

B

Byington Winery & Vineyard, Inc. 36
Byron Vineyard & Winery 26

C

Cadenasso Winery 42
Cain Cellars 79
Cakebread Cellars 75
Calera Wine Co. 35
Callaway Vineyard & Winery 16
Caparone 29
Carey Cellars 24
Carmenet Vineyard............................86
Carneros Creek Winery 70
Carrie Winery, Maurice 18
Caymus Vineyards............................78
Cedar Mountain Winery 40
Chalk Hill Winery 53
Chalone Vineyard...............................34
Chamisal Vineyard 27
Chateau Chevre..................................71
Chateau de Baun...............................50
Chateau Montelena 83
Chateau Souverain............................57
Chateau St. Jean 89
Chatom Vineyards 96
Chimney Rock Winery 67
Christian Brothers Greystone Cellars ..79
Cilurzo Vineyard and Winery.............17
Christopher Creek 52
Cline Cellars.....................................87
Clos du Bois.....................................55
Clos du Muriel.................................18
Clos du Val Wine Company, Ltd. 67

Clos Pegase..85
Codorniu Napa 67
Concannon Vineyard 40
Conn Creek Winery 75
Corbett Canyon Vineyards.................27
Cosentino Winery................................71
Creston Vineyards & Winery 28
Culbertson Winery 17
Cuvaison 85

D

David Bruce Winery 40
Davis Bynum Winery.........................52
Deer Park Escondido...........................16
Dehlinger Winery 48
Delicato Vineyards..............................95
De Loach Vineyards............................48
De Moor Winery 74
Devlin Wine Cellars............................37
Domaine Carneros.......................66, 69
Domaine Chandon 71
Domaine St. George Winery &
    Vineyards 53
Dry Creek Vineyard............................55
Dunnewood Vineyards & Winery 61

E

Eberle Winery 29
Edna Valley Vineyard 27
Emilio Guglielmo Winery 39

F

Fenestra Winery 42
Ferrara Winery 16
Ferrari-Carano Vineyards 53
Ferrer Champagne Caves, Gloria 87
Fetzer Vineyards..................................58
Ficklin Vineyards 91
Field Stone Winery 53
Filippi Vintage Co., J 19
Filsinger Vineyards..............................17
Firestone Vineyard 25
Fisher Vineyards..................................90
Flora Springs Wine Company.............80
Folie a Deux Winery 83
Foppiano Vineyards 53
Fortino Winery 37
Franciscan Vineyards 75
Frasinetti Winery 96
Freemark Abbey Winery......................80
Frey Vineyards.....................................62

Fritz Winery, J 58
Frog's Leap Winery 80

G

Gainey Vineyard 24
Galleano Winery..................................18
Geyser Peak Winery.............................56
Girard Winery......................................73
Giumarra Vineyards 92
Glen Ellen Winery...............................88
Gloria Ferres Champagne Caves 87
Gold Mine Winery................................97
Granite Springs Winery....................100
Greenstone Winery..............................98
Greenwood Ridge Vineyards 59
Grgich Hills Cellar...............................75
Groth Vineyards and Winery 73
Guenoc Winery....................................85
Guglielmo Winery, Emilio 39
Gundlach-Bundschu Winery 87

H

Hallcrest Vineyards.............................36
Handley Cellars...................................59
Hart Winery 17
Hess Collection, The 69
Hecker Pass Winery 38
Heitz Wine Cellars...............................83
Hidden Cellars 61
Hop Kiln Winery, The 56
Hope Farms Winery 29
Husch Vineyards 59

I

Indian Rock Vineyard...........................97
Inglenook-Napa Valley........................75
Iron Horse Vineyards 49

J

J. Filippi Vintage Co. 19
J. Fritz Winery 58
J. Lohr Winery 39
J. Pedroncelli Winery 57
Jackson Valley Vineyards....................98
Jaeger Winery, Thomas........................16
Jekel Vineyards 34
John Piconi Vineyard & Winery 18
Johnson's Alexander Valley Wines 54
Joseph Phelps Vineyards 82
Justin Vineyards and Winery 30

K

Kautz Vineyards 96
Keenan Winery, Robert 80
Kendall-Jackson Winery 62
Kenwood Vineyards 90
Kirigin Cellars 38
Konocti Winery 62
Korad Estate Winery 62
Korbel Champagne Cellars 49
Charles Krug Winery 80
Kruse Winery, Thomas 38

L

Lakespring Winery 71
Landmark Vineyards 90
Lazy Creek Vineyards..........................59
Leeward Winery....................................22
Live Oaks Winery 38
Livermore Valley Cellars 41
Lohr Winery, J. 39
Long Vineyards 81
Louis M. Martini 81
Lucas Winery, The...............................95
Lytton Springs Winery........................54

M

Madroña Vineyards.............................100
Maison Deutz Winery 26
Markham Vineyards.............................83
Mark West Vineyards 50
Martin Brothers Winery 30
Martini & Prati, Inc. 50
Martini, Louis M. 81
Mastantuono Winery 28
Matanzas Creek Winery......................88
Maurice Carrie Winery 18
Mayacamas Vineyards.........................69
Mazzocco Vineyards 54
McDowell Valley Vineyards 58
Meridian Vineyards..............................30
Merryvale Vineyards at Sunny
    St.Helena Winery 81
Milano Winery......................................58
Mill Creek Vineyards 56
Milliaire Winery 97
Mirassou Champagne Cellars 39
Mirassou Vineyards 39
Mission View Vineyards and Winery..30
Mondavi Winery, Robert.....................73
Monterey Vineyard 35
Monteviña 99

Monticello Cellars 69
Mont. St. John Cellars.........................69
Mosby Winery at Vega Vineyards 23
Mount Eden Vineyards 40
Mount Palomar Winery 17
Mount Veeder Winery (see Franciscan)
Mumm Napa Valley.............................76
Murphy-Goode Estate Winery 57
Murrieta's Well 41

N

Napa Creek Winery.............................81
Navarro Vineyards 60
Nervo Winery..57
Nevada City Winery 100
Newton Vineyard..................................81
Nichelini Vineyard 76
Nonini Winery, A.................................91

O

Oak Ridge Vineyards 96
Obester Winery (Half Moon Bay) 43
Obester Winery (Philo) 60
Old Creek Ranch Winery...................22

P

Page Mill Winery................................42
Parducci Wine Cellars 60
Parker Winery 26
Pastori Winery 50
Pecota Winery, Robert 85
Pedrizzetti Winery 39
Pedroncelli Winery, J. 57
Peju Province 76
Perry Creek Vineyards 100
Pesenti Winery 28
Phelps Vineyards, Joseph 82
Piconi Winery, John 18
Pine Ridge Winery 71
Piper Sonoma Cellars..........................50
Prager Winery 82
Preston Vineyards 54

Q

Quady 91
Quivira Vineyards 54

R

Rancho Sisquoc Winery 26
Rapazzini Winery.................................38
Ravenswood 87

Raymond Vineyard and Cellar 82
Retzlaff Vineyards 41
Ridge Vineyards 40
Robert Koenan Winery.......................80
Robert Mondavi Winery......................73
Robert Pecota Winery 85
Robert Sinskey Vineyards...................72
Robert Stemmler Vineyards 56
Rochioli Vineyards & Winery...............56
Rodney Strong Vineyards 51
Roederer Estate 60
Rosenblum Cellars 41
Ross-Keller Winery 26
Roudon-Smith Vineyards 36
Round Hill Winery 77
Rutherford Hill Winery 77
Rutherford Vintners..............................78

S

S. Anderson Vineyard..........................70
St. Andrew's Vineyard.........................70
St. Clement Vineyards.........................82
St. Francis Winery...............................90
St. Supéry Vineyards & Winery 77
Saintsbury...70
San Antonio Winery, Inc....................18
Sanford Winery...................................24
Santa Barbara Winery.........................23
Santa Cruz Mountain Vineyard..........37
Santa Ynez Winery 24
Santino Wines 98
Sarah's Vineyard 38
Sattui Winery, V 83, 84
Sausal Winery......................................56
Scharffenberger Cellars.......................60
Schramsberg Vineyards.......................85
Sea Ridge Winery 50
Sebastiani Vineyards...........................88
Sequoia Grove Vineyards 77
Shafer Vineyards 72
Shenandoah Vineyards........................98
Sierra Vista Winery 100
Silver Mountain Vineyards.................37
Silver Oak Wine Cellars.....................74
Silverado Vineyards 72
Simi Winery, Inc.................................55
Sinskey Vineyards, Robert 72
Smith & Hook 35
Smith-Madrone Vineyards 82
Sobon Estate 99
Sonoma-Cutrer Vineyards 51
Stag's Leap Wine Cellars 72

Stemmler Winery, Robert 56
Sterling Vineyards...............................86
Stevenot Winery..................................97
Stonegate Winery 86
StoneRidge..99
Stony Hill Vineyard............................83
Stony Ridge Winery.............................42
Storrs Winery 37
Strong Vineyards, Rodney 51
Sullivan Vineyards Winery.................78
Sutter Home Winery, Inc. 83
Sycamore Farms Natural Herb Farm (see Adelaida Cellars)

T

Talley Vineyards 27
Thomas Jaeger Winery........................16
Thomas Kruse Winery 38
Tijsseling Vineyards............................60
Topolos at Russian River Vineyards...50
Trefethen Vineyards............................70
Trentadue Winery................................58
Tudal Winery 83
Twin Hills Winery 30
Tyland Vineyards 60

V

V. Sattui Winery..........................83, 84
Valley of the Moon Winery................89
Vichon Winery 74
Villa Mt. Eden Winery 74

W

Weibel Vineyards.................................42
Weibel Winery......................................62
Wente Bros. Estate Winery 42
Wheeler Winery, William 55
White Oak Vineyards 55
Wild Horse Winery 28
William Wheeler Winery 55
Woodside Vineyards 43

Y

Yankee Hill Winery 97
York Mountain Winery 28

Z

Zaca Mesa Winery 25
ZD Wines 78

Index to Advertisers

Ritz Carlton ....Dana Point.......................Back Cover

Santa Barbara B&B Inn Keepers Guild ....Santa Barbara....................................23

For information about placing and advertisement in Automobile Club of Southern California publications, please contact:

> **Karen Clyne or Ginger Nichols**
> **Publication Sales**
> Automobile Club of Southern California
> P.O. Box 2890
> Los Angeles, CA 90051
> **Phone: (213) 741-3571 • Fax: (213) 741-3489**

Notes

Notes

THE WORLD OF WINES FESTIVAL

A TRADITION THAT IMPROVES WITH AGE

Every year, in the Fall, wine lovers from all over the nation gather to enjoy fine wines and superb cuisine in the warmth and graciousness of The Ritz-Carlton, Laguna Niguel.

Our Five-Star, Five-Diamond hotel, high on a bluff overlooking the Pacific, is continually ranked among the top resorts in the world. So it's no wonder the festival has earned a reputation as the nation's most elegant and fun-filled wine event.

Each day of the three-day Festival will feature informative seminars and tastings. Festival events include: the Future and Library Tasting; the Gre American Tasting Spectacular where over 100 prominent wineries will uncork their finest; and much more.

It's a great way to me and learn from some of t most knowledgeable experts in the world.

For more informatio call The Ritz-Carlton, Laguna Niguel at (714) 240-2000.

THE RITZ-CARLTON
LAGUNA NIGUEL

33533 Ritz-Carlton Drive, Dana Point, CA 92629   714-240-2000

43109
50595

9 781564 131829

10-3

ISBN 1-56413-182-3